Ansible Playbook Essentials

Design automation blueprints using Ansible's playbooks
to orchestrate and manage your multitier infrastructure

Gourav Shah

[PACKT] open source✲
PUBLISHING   community experience distilled

BIRMINGHAM - MUMBAI

Ansible Playbook Essentials

First published: August 2015

Production reference: 1290715

Published by Packt Publishing Ltd.
Livery Place
35 Livery Street
Birmingham B3 2PB, UK.

ISBN 978-1-78439-829-3

www.packtpub.com

Credits

Author
Gourav Shah

Reviewers
Ajey Gore
Olivier Korver
Ben Mildren
Aditya Patawari

Acquisition Editor
Vinay Argekar

Content Development Editor
Amey Varangaonkar

Technical Editor
Abhishek R. Kotian

Copy Editors
Pranjali Chury
Neha Vyas

Project Coordinator
Suzanne Coutinho

Proofreader
Safis Editing

Indexer
Monica Ajmera Mehta

Graphics
Jason Monteiro

Production Coordinator
Nilesh R. Mohite

Cover Work
Nilesh R. Mohite

About the Author

Gourav Shah (www.gouravshah.com) has extensive experience in building and managing highly available, automated, fault-tolerant infrastructure and scaling it. He started his career as a passionate Linux and open source enthusiast, transformed himself into an operations engineer, and evolved to be a cloud and DevOps expert and trainer.

In his previous avatar, Gourav headed IT operations for Efficient Frontier (now Adobe), India. He founded Initcron Systems (www.initcron.com), a niche consulting firm that specializes in DevOps enablement and cloud infrastructure management. Under the Initcron banner, he helps companies design DevOps strategies and helps implement them. Initcron also provides automation services for start-ups, as well as large enterprises.

Gourav is a coveted corporate trainer and has trained professionals from top IT companies around the world, such as IBM, CISCO, Qualcomm, Accenture, Dreamworks, Walmart Labs, Intuit, and Wells Fargo, to name a few. He runs a specialized training school by the name School of Devops (www.schoolofdevops.com) to groom world class cloud and DevOps professionals.

Acknowledgments

My journey to becoming a DevOps expert, a trainer, an entrepreneur, and with this book, an author, is full of interesting stories, people, and experiences. The seeds for my professional expertise were sown during my engineering days, when I was introduced to the open, friendly, and limitless world of free software by evangelists such as Trevor Warren, Dinesh Shah, and Dr. Nagarjuna G, with support and encouragement of a few seniors, especially Gurpreet Singh. I took Linux as a passion and quickly became the point man for any queries on computer networks and Linux.

I feel extremely fortunate to have converted my passion into a profession. My long stint at Efficient Frontier (now Adobe) has been the cornerstone of my technical foundation. It was an ocean of knowledge with great minds at work. I am honored to have worked alongside and learn from experts, namely Harold Barker, Alex Eulenberg, David Gould, and Anand Ranganathan, from whom I learned various aspects of IT Operational practices. I would like to thank Vikram Vijayaraghavan, Harold Sasaki, and Mohan Gopalakrishanan, who truly empowered me and showed me how to lead. I would also like to thank Ashok and Dennis for being great teammates.

I am deeply indebted to Michael DeHaan, the creator of the Ansible project, and the community members who have contributed toward developing, implementing, documenting, and evangelizing such a fantastic product, that is, Ansible. Without their efforts, this book would have been impossible.

I would like to thank the editing, publishing, and reviewing teams, especially Amey Varangaonkar, Abhishek Kotian, and Vinay Argekar, with whom I have been interacting, and the numerous other contributors working behind the scenes. Thank you for being extremely patient and flexible, accommodating my busy schedules, bringing me back on track, and helping me through the process toward the completion of this book. The job of reviewers is not easy. I especially thank Oliver, Ajey, Aditya, and Ben for thoroughly reviewing my work and coming up with invaluable suggestions that contributed toward improving the quality of this book significantly.

Most importantly, I would like to mention my family, which includes my parents, Rajul and Jawahar; my wife, Khushboo; my sister, Swarada; and my brother-in-law, Mayuresh, who have stood by me through thick and thin and love me unconditionally. I must thank Khushboo, my loving wife, who has supported me in all my ventures.

I dedicate this book to my father, Dr. Jawahar Shah, the most positive person I have ever met in my life, who bravely fought the battle against a formidable foe, ALS, and survived. You are my hero, Pappa!

About the Reviewers

Ajey Gore has more than 18 years of work experience in core technology strategy, research and development, and consulting. He has advised others on as well as built better business technologies for various clients across the globe while serving as the head of technology for ThoughtWorks, India.

He founded CodeIgnition (`http://codeignition.co`), a boutique DevOps and infrastructure automation firm in 2013, where he serves as the chief executive officer and principal technology consultant. Since 2013, the company has grown to 30 people. This company serves start-ups and helps them grow their business without worrying about infrastructure or scaling issues.

He is passionate about infrastructure automation, continuous delivery, the DevOps culture and tools, cloud infrastructure orchestration, virtualization strategies and hybrid cloud implementations, and networks and security. He speaks at various conferences and meetups and writes about different subjects on his website at `http://ajeygore.in`.

Since 2010, Ajey has helped to run RubyConf India, DevOpsDays India, and RailsGirls India. He is part of the Emerging Technologies Trust, a nonprofit organization responsible for running conferences, and is also committed to promoting technology in India.

Olivier Korver has been a Linux Sysadmin for over 5 years and has a passion for automation. His motto is that any repetitive task can and should be automated. Therefore, not only does he code his own middleware and OS stack in Ansible or Puppet, but he also assists developers in greatly improving their workflow by showing them how it takes very little time to set up Ansible, Docker, and Puppet and also learn the tools provided by them.

Aditya Patawari is a systems engineer by profession and just loves to play around with Linux and other open source technologies. He works on various parts of system life cycles and handles infrastructure automation and the scaling of applications. He is also a contributor to the Fedora project and can be heard talking about it along with Linux systems automation at several conferences and events. He has worked on Ansible both as part of the Fedora project and at BrowserStack, where he leads a team of systems engineers.

I would like to thank my family for being patient with me. I would also like to thank my colleagues at BrowserStack for their support and my fellow contributors at the Fedora project, who taught me so much. Lastly, a big thanks to all my friends for being there for me when I just could not manage it all.

www.PacktPub.com

Support files, eBooks, discount offers, and more

For support files and downloads related to your book, please visit www.PacktPub.com.

Did you know that Packt offers eBook versions of every book published, with PDF and ePub files available? You can upgrade to the eBook version at www.PacktPub.com and as a print book customer, you are entitled to a discount on the eBook copy. Get in touch with us at service@packtpub.com for more details.

At www.PacktPub.com, you can also read a collection of free technical articles, sign up for a range of free newsletters and receive exclusive discounts and offers on Packt books and eBooks.

https://www2.packtpub.com/books/subscription/packtlib

Do you need instant solutions to your IT questions? PacktLib is Packt's online digital book library. Here, you can search, access, and read Packt's entire library of books.

Why subscribe?

- Fully searchable across every book published by Packt
- Copy and paste, print, and bookmark content
- On demand and accessible via a web browser

Free access for Packt account holders

If you have an account with Packt at www.PacktPub.com, you can use this to access PacktLib today and view 9 entirely free books. Simply use your login credentials for immediate access.

Table of Contents

Preface

With the evolution of cloud computing, agile development methodologies, and explosion of data in recent years, there is a growing need to manage infrastructure at scale. DevOps tools and practices have become a necessity to automate every stage of such a scalable, dynamic, and complex infrastructure. Configuration management tools are at the core of this devops tool set.

Ansible is a simple, efficient, fast configuration management, orchestration and application deployment tool all combined into one. This book helps you to get familiar with writing Playbooks, Ansible's automation language. This book follows a hands-on approach to show you how to create flexible, dynamic, reusable, and data-driven roles. It then takes you through the advanced features of Ansible, such as node discovery, clustering, securing data with vault, and managing environments, and finally shows you how to use Ansible to orchestrate multitier infrastructure stack.

What this book covers

Chapter 1, Blueprinting Your Infrastructure, will introduced you to Playbooks, YAML, and so on. You will also learn about the components of a playbook.

Chapter 2, Going Modular with Ansible Roles, will demonstrate creating modular reusable automation code using Ansible roles, which are units of automation.

Chapter 3, Separating Code and Data – Variables, Facts, and Templates, covers the creation of flexible, customizable, data-driven roles with templates and variables. You will also learn about auto-discovered variables, that is, facts.

Chapter 4, Bringing In Your Code – Custom Commands and Scripts, covers bringing in your existing scripts and invoking Shell commands with Ansible.

Chapter 5, Controlling Execution Flow – Conditionals, discusses the control structures offered by Ansible to change the direction of execution.

Chapter 6, Iterative Control Structures – Loops, demonstrates how to iterate over arrays, hashes, and so on, using omnipotent with statements.

Chapter 7, Node Discovery and Clustering, discusses the discovery of topology information and creates dynamic configurations using magic variables and facts caching.

Chapter 8, Encrypting Data with Vault, discusses secure variables stored in, and shared with, version control systems using Ansible-vault.

Chapter 9, Managing Environments, covers the creation and management of isolated environments with Ansible and mapping automation code to the software development workflow.

Chapter 10, Orchestrating Infrastructure with Ansible, covers the orchestration features of Ansible, such as rolling updates, pre-tasks and post-tasks, tags, building tests into the playbook, and so on.

What you need for this book

This book assumes that you have a working installation of Ansible and a good knowledge of Linux/Unix environments and systems operations, and that you are familiar working with the command-line interface.

Who this book is for

The target audience for this book are systems or automation engineers with a few years of experience in managing various parts of infrastructure, including operating systems, application configurations, and deployments. This book also targets anyone who intends to manage systems and application configurations effectively and in an automated way, with the shortest learning curve.

It is assumed that readers have a conceptual understanding of Ansible, have already installed it and are familiar with basic operations such as creating inventory file and running ad hoc commands with Ansible.

Conventions

In this book, you will find a number of styles of text that distinguish between different kinds of information. Here are some examples of these styles, and an explanation of their meaning.

Code words in text are shown as follows: "We can include other contexts through the use of the `include` directive."

A block of code is set as follows:

```
---
# site.yml : This is a sitewide playbook
- include: www.yml
```

Any command-line input or output is written as follows:

```
$ ansible-playbook simple_playbook.yml -i customhosts
```

New terms and **important words** are shown in bold. Words that you see on the screen, in menus or dialog boxes for example, appear in the text like this: "The resultant variable hash should contain items from **defaults** plus the overridden values from **vars**".

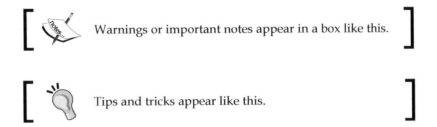

Warnings or important notes appear in a box like this.

Tips and tricks appear like this.

Reader feedback

Feedback from our readers is always welcome. Let us know what you think about this book—what you liked or may have disliked. Reader feedback is important for us to develop titles that you really get the most out of.

To send us general feedback, simply send an e-mail to feedback@packtpub.com, and mention the book title via the subject of your message.

If there is a topic that you have expertise in and you are interested in either writing or contributing to a book, see our author guide on www.packtpub.com/authors.

Customer support

Now that you are the proud owner of a Packt book, we have a number of things to help you to get the most from your purchase.

Downloading the example code

You can download the example code files for all Packt books you have purchased from your account at http://www.packtpub.com. If you purchased this book elsewhere, you can visit http://www.packtpub.com/support and register to have the files e-mailed directly to you.

Errata

Although we have taken every care to ensure the accuracy of our content, mistakes do happen. If you find a mistake in one of our books—maybe a mistake in the text or the code—we would be grateful if you would report this to us. By doing so, you can save other readers from frustration and help us improve subsequent versions of this book. If you find any errata, please report them by visiting http://www.packtpub.com/submit-errata, selecting your book, clicking on the **errata submission form** link, and entering the details of your errata. Once your errata are verified, your submission will be accepted and the errata will be uploaded on our website, or added to any list of existing errata, under the Errata section of that title. Any existing errata can be viewed by selecting your title from http://www.packtpub.com/support.

Piracy

Piracy of copyright material on the Internet is an ongoing problem across all media. At Packt, we take the protection of our copyright and licenses very seriously. If you come across any illegal copies of our works, in any form, on the Internet, please provide us with the location address or website name immediately so that we can pursue a remedy.

Please contact us at copyright@packtpub.com with a link to the suspected pirated material.

We appreciate your help in protecting our authors, and our ability to bring you valuable content.

Questions

You can contact us at questions@packtpub.com if you are having a problem with any aspect of the book, and we will do our best to address it.

Setting Up the Learning Environment

To use this book most effectively and to examine, run, and write code that is part of exercises supplied in this book, it's essential to set up a learning environment. Even though Ansible can work with any type of nodes, virtual machines, cloud servers, or bare metal hosts with an operating system installed and SSH service running, the preferred mode is to use virtual machines.

In this session, we will cover the following topics:

- Understanding the learning environment
- Understanding the pre requisites
- Installing and configuring virtualbox and vagrant
- Creating virtual machines
- Installing Ansible
- Using the sample code

Understanding the learning environment

We assume that most of our learners would like to set up the environment locally, and thus recommend using the open source and freely available software VirtualBox and Vagrant, which have support for most of the desktop operating systems, including Windows, OSX, and Linux.

The ideal setup includes five virtual machines, the purpose of which is explained as follows. You can also consolidate some of the services, for example, the load balancer and web server can be the same host:

- **Controller**: This is the only host that needs to have Ansible installed, and works as a controller. This is used to launch the `ansible-playbook` commands from the controller.

- **Database (Ubuntu)**: This host is configured with Ansible to run the MySQL database service and runs the Ubuntu distribution of Linux.

- **Database (CentOS)**: This host is configured with Ansible to run the MySQL database service, however, it runs the CentOS distribution of Linux. This is added to test multiplatform support while writing the MySQL role for Ansible.

- **Web Server**: This host is configured with Ansible to run the Apache web server application.

- **Load balancer**: This host gets configured with the haproxy application, which is an open source HTTP proxy service. This host acts as a load balancer, which accepts HTTP requests and spreads the load across available web servers.

Prerequisites

For most up-to-date instructions on prerequisites, software and hardware requirements, as well as setup instructions, refer to the following GitHub repository:

`https://github.com/schoolofdevops/ansible-playbook-essentials.`

Systems prerequisites

A moderately configured desktop or a laptop system should be sufficient to set up the learning environment. The following are the recommended prerequisites in the context of of software and hardware:

Processor	2 cores
Memory	2.5 GB RAM available
Disk Space	20 GB of free space
Operating System	Windows, OS X (Mac), Linux

The base software

For the purpose of setting up the learning environment, we recommend using the following software:

- **VirtualBox**: Oracle's virtualbox is a desktop virtualization software, which is freely available. It works on a variety of operating systems, including Windows, OS X, Linux, FreeBSD, Solaris, and so on. It provides a layer of hypervisor and allows one to create and run virtual machines on top of an existing base OS. The code provided along with this book has been tested on 4.3x versions of virtualbox. However, any version of virtualbox, which is compatible with the vagrant version can be used.

- **Vagrant**: This is a tool that allows one to easily create and share virtual environments on most hypervisors and cloud platforms, including but not limited to virtualbox. It can automate tasks such as importing an image, specifying resources, such as memory and CPUs assigned to VMs, and setting up network interfaces, hostnames, user credentials, and so on. Since it provides a text configuration in the form of a Vagrant file, virtual machines can be provisioned programmatically, making them easy to use it with other tools such as **Jenkins** to automate build and test pipelines.

- **Git for Windows**: Even though we do not intend to use Git, which is a version control software, we use this software to install the SSH utility on the Windows system. Vagrant needs an SSH binary available in the path. Windows is not packaged with the SSH utility, and Git for Windows is the easiest way to install it on Windows. Alternative options such as **Cygwin** exist.

The following table lists the version OS the software used to develop the code provided with the book, with download links:

Software	Version	Download URI
VirtualBox	4.3.30	`https://www.virtualbox.org/wiki/Downloads`
Vagrant	1.7.3	`https://www.vagrantup.com/downloads.html`
Git for Windows	1.9.5	`https://git-scm.com/download/win`

Learners are advised to download, install, and refer to the respective documentation pages to get familiar with these tools before proceeding.

Creating virtual machines

Once you have installed the base software, you can use vagrant to bring up the virtual machines required. Vagrant uses a specification file by the name Vagrantfile, a sample of which is as follows:

```ruby
# -*- mode: ruby -*-
# vi: set ft=ruby :
# Sample Vagranfile to setup Learning Environment
# for Ansible Playbook Essentials

VAGRANTFILE_API_VERSION = "2"
Vagrant.configure(VAGRANTFILE_API_VERSION) do |config|
  config.vm.box = "ansible-ubuntu-1204-i386"
  config.vm.box_url = "https://cloud-
  images.ubuntu.com/vagrant/precise/current/precise-server-
  cloudimg-i386-vagrant-disk1.box"
  config.vm.define "control" do |control|
    control.vm.network :private_network, ip: "192.168.61.10"
  end
  config.vm.define "db" do |db|
    db.vm.network :private_network, ip: "192.168.61.11"
  end
  config.vm.define "dbel" do |db|
    db.vm.network :private_network, ip: "192.168.61.14"
    db.vm.box = "opscode_centos-6.5-i386"
    db.vm.box = "http://opscode-vm-
    bento.s3.amazonaws.com/vagrant/virtualbox/opscode_centos-
    6.5_chef-provisionerless.box"
  end
  config.vm.define "www" do |www|
    www.vm.network :private_network, ip: "192.168.61.12"
  end
  config.vm.define "lb" do |lb|
    lb.vm.network :private_network, ip: "192.168.61.13"
  end
end
```

The preceding Vagrant file contains specifications to set up five virtual machines, as described in the beginning of this chapter, which are, control, db, dbel, www, and lb.

Learners are advised to use following instructions to create and start the virtual machines required to set up the learning environment:

1. Create a directory structure for the learning environment setup, for example, `learn/ansible`, anywhere on the system:

2. Copy the `Vagrantfile` file provided previously to the `learn/ansible` directory. The tree should now look as follows:

```
learn
  \_ ansible
       \_ Vagrantfile
```

 The `Vagrantfile` file contains specifications for the virtual machines described in the earlier section.

3. Open a terminal and go to `learn/ansible`.

4. Bring up the control node and log in to it, as folloes:

    ```
    $ vagrant up control
    $ vagrant ssh control
    ```

5. From a separate terminal window, from the `learn/ansible` directory, bring up the remaining virtual machine, one at a time, as follows:

    ```
    $ vagrant up db
    $ vagrant up www
    $ vagrant up lb
    optionally (for centos based mysql configurations)
    $ vagrant up dbel
    Optionally, to login to to the virtual machines as
    $ vagrant ssh db
    $ vagrant ssh www
    $ vagrant ssh lb
    optionally (for centos based mysql configurations)
    $ vagrant ssh dbel
    ```

Installing Ansible on the controller

Once the virtual machines are created and brought up, Ansible needs to be installed on the controller. Since Ansible is agentless and manages nodes using SSH transport, no additional setup is needed on the nodes except for ensuring that the SSH service is running. To install Ansible on the controller, refer to the following steps. These instructions are specific to the Ubuntu distribution of Linux, as that's what we use on our controller. For generic installation instructions, please refer to the following page:

```
http://docs.ansible.com/intro_installation.html.
```

The steps are as follows:

1. Log in to the controller using the following command:

   ```
   # from inside learn/ansible directory
   $ vagrant ssh control
   ```

2. Update the repository cache using the following command:

   ```
   $ sudo apt-get update
   ```

3. Install the prerequisite software and repositories:

   ```
   # On Ubuntu 14.04 and above
   $ sudo apt-get install -y software-properties-common
   $ sudo apt-get install -y python-software-properties
   $ sudo apt-add-repository ppa:ansible/ansible
   ```

4. Update the repository cache after adding a new repository, such as follows:

   ```
   $ sudo apt-get update
   ```

5. Install Ansible using the following command:

   ```
   $ sudo apt-get install -y ansible
   ```

6. Validate Ansible using the following command:

   ```
   $ ansible --version
   [sample output]
   vagrant@vagrant:~$ ansible --version
   ansible 1.9.2
     configured module search path = None
   ```

Using sample code

The sample code provided with this book is divided as per the chapter numbers. A directory named after the chapter number contains the snapshot of the state of the code at the end of the respective chapter. Learners are advised to independently create their own code and use the sample code as a reference. Moreover, if the readers skip one or more chapters, they can use the sample code from the previous chapter as a base.

For example, while using *Chapter 6, Iterative Control Structures – Loops*, you can use the sample code from *Chapter 5, Controlling Execution Flow – Conditionals*, as a base.

Downloading the example code

You can download the example code files for all Packt books you have purchased from your account at http://www.packtpub.com. If you purchased this book elsewhere, you can visit http://www.packtpub.com/support and register to have the files e-mailed directly to you.

1
Blueprinting Your Infrastructure

This book is a primer for anyone who has conceptual knowledge of Ansible and would like to get started writing Ansible playbooks to automate common infrastructure tasks, orchestrate application deployments, and/or manage configurations across multiple environments. This book follows an incremental approach, starting with the basics such as learning about the anatomy of a playbook and writing simple roles to create modular code. Once comfortable with the basics, you will be introduced to primitives such as adding dynamic data with variables and templates, and controlling execution flow with conditionals and iterators. This is then followed by more advanced topics such as node discovery, clustering, encrypting data, and managing environments. We conclude with the discussion on the orchestration features of Ansible. Let's begin our journey towards being an Ansible practitioner by learning about playbooks.

In this chapter, we will learn about:

- The anatomy of a playbook
- What plays are and how to write a Hosts inventory and search patterns
- Ansible modules and the batteries-included approach

Getting introduced to Ansible

Ansible is a simple, flexible, and extremely powerful tool that gives you the ability to automate common infrastructure tasks, run ad hoc commands, and deploy multitier applications spanning multiple machines. Even though you can use Ansible to launch commands on a number of hosts in parallel, the real power lies in managing those using playbooks.

As systems engineer, infrastructure that we typically need to automate contains complex multitier applications. Each of which represents a class of servers, for example, load balancers, web servers, database servers, caching applications, and middleware queues. Since many of these applications have to work in tandem to provide a service, there is topology involved as well. For example, a load balancer would connect to web servers, which in turn read/write to a database and connect to the caching server to fetch in-memory objects. Most of the time, when we launch such application stacks, we need to configure these components in a very specific order.

Here is an example of a very common three-tier web application running a load balancer, a web server, and a database backend:

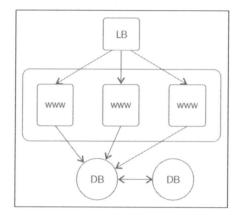

Ansible lets you translate this diagram into a blueprint, which defines your infrastructure policies. The format used to specify such policies is what playbooks are.

Example policies and the sequence in which those are to be applied is shown in the following steps:

1. Install, configure, and start the MySQL service on the database servers.
2. Install and configure the web servers that run **Nginx** with **PHP** bindings.
3. Deploy a Wordpress application on the web servers and add respective configurations to Nginx.

4. Start the Nginx service on all web servers after deploying Wordpress. Finally, install, configure, and start the **haproxy** service on the load balancer hosts. Update haproxy configurations with the hostnames of all the web servers created earlier.

The following is a sample playbook that translates the infrastructure blueprint into policies enforceable by Ansible:

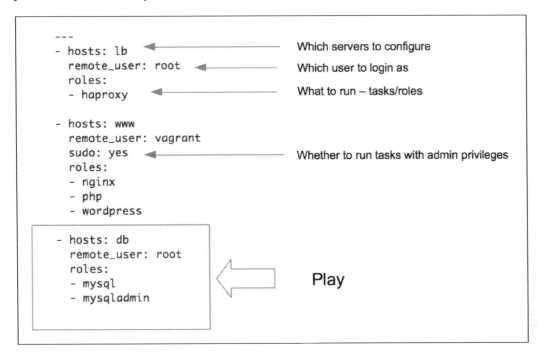

Plays

A playbook consists of one or more plays, which map groups of hosts to well-defined tasks. The preceding example contains three plays, each to configure one layer in the multitiered web application. Plays also define the order in which tasks are configured. This allows us to orchestrate multitier deployments. For example, configure the load balancers only after starting the web servers, or perform two-phase deployment where the first phase only adds this configurations and the second phase starts the services in the desired order.

YAML – the playbook language

As you may have already noticed, the playbook that we wrote previously resembles more of a text configuration than a code snippet. This is because the creators of Ansible chose to use a simple, human-readable, and familiar YAML format to blueprint the infrastructure. This adds to Ansible's appeal, as users of this tool need not learn any special programming language to get started with. Ansible code is self-explanatory and self-documenting in nature. A quick crash course on YAML should suffice to understand the basic syntax. Here is what you need to know about YAML to get started with your first playbook:

- The first line of a playbook should begin with "--- " (three hyphens) which indicates the beginning of the YAML document.

- Lists in YAML are represented with a hyphen followed by a white space. A playbook contains a list of plays; they are represented with "- ". Each play is an associative array, a dictionary, or a map in terms of key-value pairs.

- Indentations are important. All members of a list should be at the same indentation level.

- Each play can contain key-value pairs separated by ":" to denote hosts, variables, roles, tasks, and so on.

Our first playbook

Equipped with the basic rules explained previously and assuming readers have done a quick dive into YAML fundamentals, we will now begin writing our first playbook. Our problem statement includes the following:

1. Create a devops user on all hosts. This user should be part of the devops group.

2. Install the "htop" utility. **Htop** is an improved version of top—an interactive system process monitor.

3. Add the Nginx repository to the web servers and start it as a service.

Now, we will create our first playbook and save it as `simple_playbook.yml` containing the following code:

```
---
- hosts: all
  remote_user: vagrant
  sudo: yes
  tasks:
```

```
- group:
    name: devops
    state: present
- name: create devops user with admin privileges

  user:
    name: devops
    comment: "Devops User"
    uid: 2001
    group: devops
- name: install htop package
  action: apt name=htop state=present update_cache=yes

- hosts: www
  user: vagrant
  sudo: yes
  tasks:
  - name: add official nginx repository
    apt_repository:
      repo: 'deb http://nginx.org/packages/ubuntu/ lucid nginx'
  - name: install nginx web server and ensure its at the latest
    version
    apt:
      name: nginx
      state: latest
  - name: start nginx service
    service:
      name: nginx
      state: started
```

Our playbook contains two plays. Each play consists of the following two important parts:

- **What to configure**: We need to configure a host or group of hosts to run the play against. Also, we need to include useful connection information, such as which user to connect as, whether to use sudo command, and so on.
- **What to run**: This includes the specification of tasks to be run, including which system components to modify and which state they should be in, for example, installed, started, or latest. This could be represented with tasks and later on, by roles.

Let's now look at each of these briefly.

Creating a host inventory

Before we even start writing our playbook with Ansible, we need to define an inventory of all hosts that need to be configured, and make it available for Ansible to use. Later, we will start running plays against a selection of hosts from this inventory. If you have an existing inventory, such as cobbler, LDAP, a CMDB software, or wish to pull it from a cloud provider, such as ec2, it can be pulled from Ansible using the concept of a dynamic inventory.

For text-based local inventory, the default location is /etc/ansible/hosts. For our learning environment, however, we will create a custom inventory file customhosts in our working directory, the contents of which are shown as follows. You are free to create your own inventory file:

```
#customhosts
#inventory configs for my cluster
[db]
192.168.61.11   ansible_ssh_user=vagrant

[www]
www-01.example.com ansible_ssh_user=ubuntu
www-02 ansible_ssh_user=ubuntu

[lb]
lb0.example.com
```

Now, when our playbook maps a play to the group, the www (hosts: www), hosts in that group will be configured. The all keywords will match to all hosts from the inventory.

Thr following are the guidelines to for creating inventory files:

- Inventory files follow INI style configurations, which essentially include configuration blocks that start with host group/class names included in "[ ]".
  This allows the selective execution on classes of systems, for example, [namenodes].

- A single host can be part of multiple groups. In such cases, host variables from both the groups will get merged, and the precedence rules apply. We will discuss variables and precedence in detail later.

- Each group contains a list of hosts and connection details, such as the SSH user to connect as, the SSH port number if non-default, SSH credentials/keys, sudo credentials, and so on. Hostnames can also contain globs, ranges, and more, to make it easy to include multiple hosts of the same type, which follow some naming patterns.

 After creating an inventory of the hosts, it's a good idea to validate connectivity using Ansible's ping module (for example, `ansible -m ping all`).

Patterns

In the preceding playbook, the following lines decide which hosts to select to run a specific play:

```
- hosts: all
- hosts: www
```

The first code will match all hosts, and the second code will match hosts which are part of the www group.

Patterns can be any of the following or their combinations:

Pattern Types	Examples
Group name	`namenodes`
Match all	`all` or `*`
Range	`namenode[0:100]`
Hostnames/hostname globs	`*.example.com`, `host01.example.com`
Exclusions	`namenodes:!secondaynamenodes`
Intersection	`namenodes:&zookeeper`
Regular expressions	`~(nn|zk).*\.example\.org`

Tasks

Plays map hosts to tasks. Tasks are a sequence of actions performed against a group of hosts that match the pattern specified in a play. Each play typically contains multiple tasks that are run serially on each machine that matches the pattern. For example, take a look at the following code snippet:

```
- group:
    name:devops
    state: present
- name: create devops user with admin privileges
  user:
    name: devops
    comment: "Devops User"
    uid: 2001
    group: devops
```

In the preceding example, we have two tasks. The first one is to create a group, and second is to create a user and add it to the group created earlier. If you notice, there is an additional line in the second task, which starts with `name:`. While writing tasks, it's good to provide a name with a human-readable description of what this task is going to achieve. If not, the action string will be printed instead.

Each action in a task list can be declared by specifying the following:

- The name of the module
- Optionally, the state of the system component being managed
- The optional parameters

> With newer versions of Ansible (0.8 onwards), writing an action keyword is now optional. We can directly provide the name of the module instead. So, both of these lines will have a similar action, that is,. installing a package with the `apt` module:
>
> ```
> action: apt name=htop state=present update_cache=yes
> apt: name=nginx state=latest
> ```

Ansible stands out from other configuration management tools, with its batteries-included included approach. These batteries are "modules." It's important to understand what modules are before we proceed.

Modules

Modules are the encapsulated procedures that are responsible for managing specific system components on specific platforms.

Consider the following example:

- The `apt` module for Debian and the `yum` module for RedHat helps manage system packages
- The `user` module is responsible for adding, removing, or modifying users on the system
- The `service` module will start/stop system services

Modules abstract the actual implementation from users. They expose a declarative syntax that accepts a list of the parameters and states of the system components being managed. All this can be declared using the human-readable YAML syntax, using key-value pairs.

In terms of functionality, modules resemble providers for those of you who are familiar with Chef/Puppet software. Instead of writing procedures to create a user, with Ansible we declare which state our component should be in, that is, which user to create, its state, and its characteristics, such as UID, group, shell, and so on. The actual procedures are inherently known to Ansible via modules, and are executed in the background.

> The `Command` and `Shell` modules are special ones. They neither take key-value pairs as parameters, nor are idempotent.

Ansible comes preinstalled with a library of modules, which ranges from the ones which manage basic system resources to more sophisticated ones that send notifications, perform cloud integrations, and so on. If you want to provision an ec2 instance, create a database on the remote PostgreSQL server, and get notifications on **IRC**, then Ansible has a module for it. Isn't this amazing?

No need to worry about finding an external plugin, or struggle to integrate with cloud providers, and so on. To find a list of modules available, you can refer to the Ansible documentation at `http://docs.ansible.com/list_of_all_modules.html`.

Ansible is extendible too. If you do not find a module that does the job for you, it's easy to write one, and it doesn't have to be in Python. A module can be written for Ansible in the language of your choice. This is discussed in detail at `http://docs.ansible.com/developing_modules.html`.

The modules and idempotence

Idempotence is an important characteristic of a module. It is something which can be applied on your system multiple times, and will return deterministic results. It has built-in intelligence. For instance, we have a task that uses the `apt` module to install Nginx and ensure that it's up to date. Here is what happens if you run it multiple times:

- Every time idempotance is run multiple times, the `apt` module will compare what has been declared in the playbook versus the current state of that package on the system. The first time it runs, Ansible will determine that Nginx is not installed, and will go ahead with the installation.

- For every consequent run, it will skip the installation part, unless there is a new version of the package available in the upstream repositories.

This allows executing the same task multiple times without resulting in the error state. Most of the Ansible modules are idempotent, except for the command and shell modules. Users will have to make these modules idempotent.

Running the playbook

Ansible comes with the `ansible-playbook` command to launch a playbook with. Let's now run the plays we created:

```
$ ansible-playbook simple_playbook.yml -i customhosts
```

Here is what happens when you run the preceding command:

- The `ansible-playbook` parameter is the command that takes the playbook as an argument (`simple_playbook.yml`) and runs the plays against the hosts

- The `simple_playbook` parameter contains the two plays that we created: one for common tasks, and the other for installing Nginx

- The `customhosts` parameter is our host's inventory, which lets Ansible know which hosts, or groups of hosts, to call plays against

Launching the preceding command will start calling plays, orchestrating in the sequence that we described in the playbook. Here is the output of the preceding command:

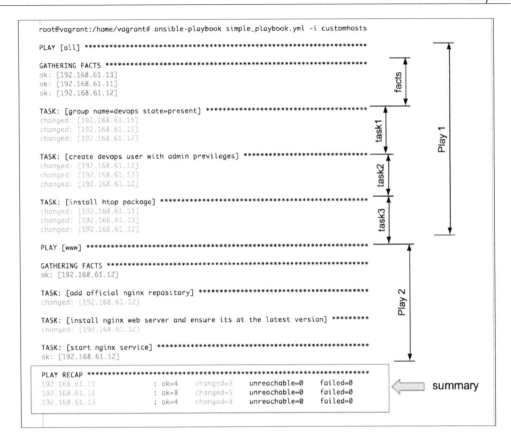

```
root@vagrant:/home/vagrant# ansible-playbook simple_playbook.yml -i customhosts

PLAY [all] **********************************************************************

GATHERING FACTS ****************************************************************
ok: [192.168.61.13]
ok: [192.168.61.11]
ok: [192.168.61.12]

TASK: [group name=devops state=present] ***************************************
changed: [192.168.61.13]
changed: [192.168.61.11]
changed: [192.168.61.12]

TASK: [create devops user with admin previleges] ******************************
changed: [192.168.61.11]
changed: [192.168.61.13]
changed: [192.168.61.12]

TASK: [install htop package] **************************************************
changed: [192.168.61.11]
changed: [192.168.61.13]
changed: [192.168.61.12]

PLAY [www] *********************************************************************

GATHERING FACTS ****************************************************************
ok: [192.168.61.12]

TASK: [add official nginx repository] *****************************************
changed: [192.168.61.12]

TASK: [install nginx web server and ensure its at the latest version] *********
changed: [192.168.61.12]

TASK: [start nginx service] ***************************************************
ok: [192.168.61.12]

PLAY RECAP ********************************************************************
192.168.61.11              : ok=4    changed=3    unreachable=0    failed=0
192.168.61.12              : ok=8    changed=5    unreachable=0    failed=0
192.168.61.13              : ok=4    changed=3    unreachable=0    failed=0
```

Let's now analyze what happened:

- Ansible reads the playbooks specified as an argument to the `ansible-playbook` command and starts executing plays in the serial order.

- The first play that we declared, runs against the "all" hosts. The `all` keyword is a special pattern that will match all hosts (similar to *). So, the tasks in the first play will be executed on all hosts in the inventory we passed as an argument.

- Before running any of the tasks, Ansible will gather information about the systems that it is going to configure. This information is collected in the form of facts.

- The first play includes the creation of the `devops` group and user, and installation of the htop package. Since we have three hosts in our inventory, we see one line per host being printed, which indicates whether there was a change in the state of the entity being managed. If the state was not changed, "ok" will be printed.

- Ansible then moves to the next play. This is executed only on one host, as we have specifed "hosts:www" in our play, and our inventory contains a single host in the group "www".

- During the second play, the Nginx repository is added, the package is installed, and the service is started.

- Finally, Ansible prints the summary of the playbook run in the "PLAY RECAP" section. It indicates how many modifications were made, if any of the hosts were unreachable, or execution failed on any of the systems.

 What if a host is unresponsive, or fails to run tasks? Ansible has built-in intelligence, which will identify such issues and take the failed host out of rotation. It will not affect the execution on other hosts.

Review questions

Do you think you've understood the chapter well enough? Try answering the following questions to test your understanding:

1. What is idempotence when it comes to modules?
2. What is the host's inventory and why is it required?
3. Playbooks map ___ to ___ (fill in the blanks)
4. What types of patterns can you use while selecting a list of hosts to run plays against?
5. Where is the actual procedure to execute an action on a specific platform defined?
6. Why is it said that Ansible comes with batteries included?

Summary

In this chapter, you learned about what Ansible playbooks are, what components those are made up of, and how to blueprint your infrastructure with it. We also did a primer on YAML—the language used to create plays. You learned about how plays map tasks to hosts, how to create a host inventory, how to filter hosts with patterns, and how to use modules to perform actions on our systems. We then created a simple playbook as a proof of concept.

In the upcoming chapter, we will start refactoring our code to create reusable and modular chunks of code, and call them roles.

2
Going Modular with Ansible Roles

In the last chapter, you learned about writing a simple playbook with Ansible. You also learned about the concepts of plays which map hosts to tasks. Writing tasks in a single playbook may work fine for a very simple setup. However, if we have multiple applications spanning across number of hosts, this will quickly become unmanageable.

In this chapter, you will be introduced to the following concepts:

- What makes a role and what are roles used for?
- How to create roles to provide abstraction?
- Organizing content to provide modularity
- Using include statements
- Writing simple tasks and handlers
- Installing packages, managing services, and serving files with Ansible modules

Understanding roles

In real-life scenarios, we will mostly be configuring web servers, database servers, load balancers, middleware queues, and so on. If you take one step back and look at the big picture, you will realize that you are configuring groups of identical servers in a repeatable fashion.

To manage such infrastructures in the most efficient way, we need some abstraction which allows us to define what we need to configure in each of these groups, and call them by name. That's exactly what roles do. Ansible roles allow us to configure groups of nodes at the same time, without repeating ourselves. Roles also provide a way to create modular code, which then can then be shared and reused.

Naming roles

A common practice is to create roles that map to each application or component of your infrastructure that you would like to configure. For example:

- Nginx
- MySQL
- MongoDB
- Tomcat

The directory layout for roles

Roles are nothing but directories laid out in a specific manner. Roles follow predefined directory layout conventions and expect each component to be in the path meant for it.

The following is an example of a role, called Nginx:

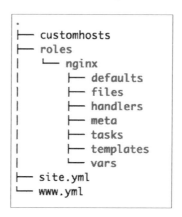

Let's now look at the rules of the game and what each of the components in the preceding diagram is for:

- Each role contains a directory which is named after itself, for example, Nginx, with `roles/` as its parent directory. Each named role directory contains one or more optional subdirectories. The most common subdirectories to be present are tasks, templates, and handlers. Each of these subdirectories typically contain the `main.yml` file, which is a default file.

- Tasks contain the core logic, for example, they will have code specifications to install packages, start services, manage files, and so on. If we consider a role to be a movie, a task would be the protagonist.

- Tasks alone cannot do everything. Considering our analogy with movies, it's incomplete without the supporting cast. Protagonists have friends, cars, lovers, and antagonists to complete the story. Similarly, tasks consume data, call for static or dynamic files, trigger actions, and so on. That's where files, handlers, templates, defaults, and `vars` come in. Let's look at what these are for.

- Vars and defaults provide data about your application/role, for example, which port your server should run on, the path for storing the application data, which user to run the service as, and so on. Default variables were introduced in version 1.3 and these allow us to provide sane defaults. These can later be overridden from other places, for example, `vars`, `group_vars`, and `host_vars`. Variables are merged and precedence rules apply. This gives us a lot of flexibility to configure our servers selectively. For example, running the web server on port `80` on all hosts except for the ones in the staging environment, which should run it on port `8080`.

- Files and templates subdirectories provide options for managing files. Typically, the files subdirectory is used to copy over static files to destination hosts, for example, some application installers archive static text files, and so on. In addition to static files, frequently you may need to manage files that are are generated on the fly. For example, a configuration file that has parameters such as port, user, and memory, which can be provided dynamically using variables. Generating such files requires a special type of primitive, called templates.

- Tasks can trigger actions based on the change of a state or a condition. In a movie, the protagonist may chase the antagonist and take revenge based on the provocation or an event. An example event is kidnapping the protagonist's lady love. Similarly, you may need to perform an action on your hosts, for example, restarting a service based on what happened earlier, which could be a change in the state of a configuration file. This trigger-action relationship can be specified using a handler.

Continuing our analogy, many popular movies have sequels and sometimes even prequels. In such cases, one should watch it in a particular order, as the storyline of a sequel depends on something that happened in the previous movie. Similarly, a role can have a dependency on another role. A very common example is, before installing Tomcat, Java should be present on the system. These dependencies are defined in the meta subdirectory of a role.

Let's get hands-on with this by creating a role for the Nginx application. Let's take a problem statement, try to solve it, and learn about roles in the process.

Consider the following scenario. With the onset of the soccer world cup, we need to create a web server to serve up a page on sports news.

Being a follower of agile methodologies, we will do this in phases. In the first phase, we will just install a web server and serve up a home page. Let's now break this down into the steps we need to take to achieve this:

1. Install a web server. In this case, we will use 'Nginx' as it is a lightweight web server.

2. Manage configuration for the Nginx web server.

3. Start the web server after installing it.

4. Copy over an HTML file, which will be served as a home page.

Now that we have identified what steps to take, we also need to map them to the respective module types we will use to achieve each of these:

- Installing Nginx = Package module (apt)
- Configuring Nginx = File module (file)
- Starting Nginx = Systems module (service)
- Serve Webpage = Files module (file)

Before we start writing code, we will start creating a layout to organize our files.

Creating a site-wide playbook, nesting, and using include statements

As a best practice, we will create a top-level file, which will contain the blueprint of our complete infrastructure. Technically, we can include everything that we need to configure inside just one file. However, that would have two problems:

- It would quickly get out of control as we start adding tasks, variables, and handlers to this single file. It would be a nightmare to maintain such code.

- It would also be difficult to reuse and share such code. One of the advantages of using a tool such as Ansible is its ability to separate data from code. Data is organization-specific, and code is generic. This generic code can then be shared with others. However, if you write everything in a single file, it would be impossible to do so.

To avoid this problem, we will start organizing our code in a modular fashion, as follows:

- We will create roles for each of the applications that we need to configure. In this case, it is Nginx

- Our web server may need to install more than one application in addition to Nginx, for example, PHP and OpenSSL. To encapsulate all of these, we will create a playbook named `www.yml`.

- The preceding playbook that we created will map hosts with the Nginx role. We may add more roles to it later.

- We will add this playbook to the top-level playbook, that is, `site.yml`

The following diagram depicts the preceding steps in a very simple manner:

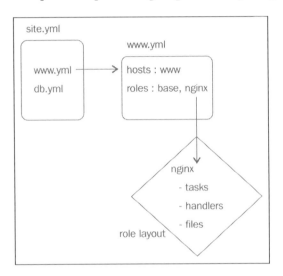

Here is our `site.yml` file:

```
---
# site.yml : This is a sitewide playbook
- include: www.yml
```

The preceding `include` directive assists us with modularizing the code. Instead of writing it all in one file, we split the logic and import what is required. In this case, we will include another playbook, which is called a **nested playbook**.

The following are some guidelines on what can be included and how:

- The `include` directive can be used to include tasks, handlers, and even other playbooks

- If you include a playbook inside another like we did in the `site.yml` file, you cannot substitute the variables

- The `include` keyword can be used in combination with regular task/handler specifications

- It's possible to pass parameters with include statements. This is called as **parameterized include**

> **Roles and auto-includes**
>
> Roles have implicit rules to auto include files. So long as you follow the directory layout conventions, you are assured that all your tasks, handlers, and the rest of the files are included automatically. Hence, it's important to create the subdirectories with the exact names as specified by Ansible.

Creating the www playbook

We created a site-wide playbook and used an include statement to call another playbook by the name `www.yml`. We will now create this file with one play, which maps our web server hosts to the Nginx role:

```
---
#www.yml : playbook for web servers
- hosts: www
  remote_user: vagrant
  sudo: yes
  roles:
    - nginx
```

The above code works as follows:

- Run this code on any host that maps to the [www] group specified in the hosts file.

- For each directory inside the `roles/nginx/*` file, include `roles/nginx/*/main.yml` to the play. This includes `tasks`, `handlers`, `vars`, `meta`, `default`, and so on. This is where the auto include rules apply.

The default and custom role paths

By default, Ansible looks inside the `roles/` subdirectory of the project that we create playbooks for. Being top-class devops engineers, we will follow the best practice to have a centralized, version-controlled repository to store all your roles. We may also end up reusing the roles created by community. Once we do this, we can reuse these roles across multiple projects. In such cases, we will check out the code at one or more locations, for example:

- `/deploy/ansible/roles`
- `/deploy/ansible/community/roles`

For nondefault paths, we will need to add the `roles_path` parameter to `ansible.cfg` as shown in the following command:

```
roles_path = /deploy/ansible/roles:/deploy/ansible/community/roles
```

Parameterizing the roles

At times, we may need to override default parameters specified inside vars or the default directory of a role, for example, running web servers on port 8080 instead of 80. In such cases, we can also pass parameters to roles in the preceding playbook, as follows:

```
---
#www.yml : playbook for web servers
- hosts: www
  roles:
- { role: nginx, port: 8080 }
```

Creating a base role

In the previous chapter, we created a simple playbook with all plays written inside the same file. After discovering new and exciting information about roles, we will start refactoring our code and making it modular.

Refactoring our code – creating a base role

We have written two plays in the `simple_playbook.yml` file. We intended to run the first play on all hosts. This play has tasks to create users, install essential packages, and
so on:

```
---
- hosts: all
  remote_user: vagrant
  sudo: yes
  tasks:
  - group: name=devops state=present
  - name: create devops user with admin previleges
    user: name=devops comment="Devops User" uid=2001 group=devops
  - name: install htop package
    action: apt name=htop state=present update_cache=yes
```

It's a good practice to combine all such essential tasks and create a base role. You can name it as base, common, essential, or whatever you please, but the concept remains the same. We will now move this code to the base role:

1. Create the directory layout for the base role. Since we are only going to specify tasks, we just need one subdirectory inside the base:

   ```
   $ mkdir -p roles/base/tasks
   ```

2. Create the `main.yml` file inside `roles/base/tasks` to specify tasks for the base role.

3. Edit the `main.yml` file and add the following code:

   ```
   ---
   # essential tasks. should run on all nodes
     - name: creating devops group
       group: name=devops state=present
     - name: create devops user
       user: name=devops comment="Devops User" uid=2001 group=devops
     - name: install htop package
       action: apt name=htop state=present update_cache=yes
   ```

Creating an Nginx role

We will now create a separate role for Nginx and move the previous code that we wrote in the `simple_playbook.yml` file to it, as follows:

1. Create the directory layout for the Nginx role:

   ```
   $ mkdir roles/nginx
   $ cd roles/nginx
   $ mkdir tasks meta files
   $ cd tasks
   ```

2. Create the `install.yml` file inside `roles/base`. Move the Nginx-related tasks to it. It should look like this:

   ```
   ---

   - name: add official nginx repository
     apt_repository: repo='deb
     http://nginx.org/packages/ubuntu/ lucid nginx'
   - name: install nginx web server and ensure its at the
     latest version
     apt: name=nginx state=latest force=yes
   ```

3. We will also create the `service.yml` file to manage the state of the Nginx daemon:

   ```
   ---

   - name: start nginx service
     service: name=nginx state=started
   ```

4. We looked at the `include` directive earlier. We will use it to include both the `install.yml` and `service.yml` files in the `main.yml` file, as follows:

   ```
   ---

   # This is main tasks file for nginx role
     - include: install.yml
   - include: service.yml
   ```

> **Best Practice**
>
> Why are we creating multiple files to hold the code that installs packages and manages services, separately? That's because well-factored roles allow you to selectively enable specific features. For example, at times, you may want to deploy services in multiple phases. In the first phase, you may just want to install and configure applications, and start services only in the second phase of your deployment. In such cases, having modular tasks can help. You can always include them all in the `main.yml` file.

Adding role dependencies

We have some essential tasks specified in the base role. We may keep on adding more tasks which are a prerequisite for the applications that follow. In such cases, we would like our Nginx role to be dependent on the base role. We will now specify this dependency inside the meta subdirectory. Let's take a look at the following steps:

1. Create the `main.yml` file inside the `roles/nginx/meta/main.yml` path.

2. Add the following code to the `main.yml` file inside the `meta` directory:

   ```
   ---
   dependencies:
     - {role: base}
   ```

The preceding specification will ensure that the base role is always applied before any task in Nginx starts running.

Managing files for Nginx

As per our solution to the scenario, we already have Ansible tasks to install Nginx and to start the service. We still don't have a web page to serve yet, and we did not think about the Nginx site configurations. We don't expect Nginx to magically know about how and where to serve the web page from, do we?

We need to perform the following steps to serve the HTML page:

1. Create a site configuration that lets Nginx know which port to listen to for requests, and what to do when a request comes.

2. Create some HTML content, which will be served when an HTTP request comes in.

3. Add code to `tasks/main.yml` to copy over these files.

You might have noticed, both steps 1 and 2 require that you create and manage some files on the host, which will run the Nginx web server. You also learned about the file and the subdirectory of a role. You guessed it right. We will use this subdirectory to host our files and have them copied over to all the Nginx hosts with Ansible. So, let's create these files now using the following command:

```
$ cd roles/nginx/files
```

Create a `default.configuration` file to manage the default Nginx site configurations.
This file should contain parameters such as port, server name, and web root configurations, as follows:

```
#filename: roles/nginx/files/default.conf
server {
  listen 80;
  server_name localhost;
  location / {
    root /usr/share/nginx/html;
    index index.html;
  }
}
```

We will also create an `index.html` file, which we will push to all web servers:

```
#filename: roles/nginx/files/indx.html
<html>
  <body>
    <h1>Ole Ole Ole </h1>
    <p> Welcome to FIFA World Cup News Portal</p>
  </body>
</html>
```

Now that we have created these files, we will add tasks to copy these over and put them in `roles/nginx/tasks/configure.yml`, as follows:

```
---
  - name: create default site configurations
    copy: src=default.conf dest=/etc/nginx/conf.d/default.conf
    mode=0644
  - name: create home page for default site
    copy: src=index.html dest=/usr/share/nginx/html/index.html
```

We will also update the `main.yaml` file inside tasks to include the newly created file, and add it before the `service.yml` file:

```
---
# This is the main tasks file for the nginx role
  - include: install.yml
  - include: configure.yml
  - include: service.yml
```

Automating events and actions with handlers

Let's assume that we are managing Nginx manually, and that we have to change the port that Nginx listens to from the default site to `8080`. What would we do to make this happen? Sure, we would edit the `default.conf` file and change the port from 80 to 8080. However, would that be enough? Would that make Nginx listen to port 8080 immediately after editing this file? The answer is no. There is one more step involved. Let's take a look at the following screenshot:

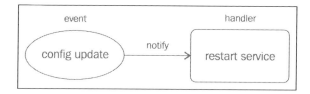

When we change a configuration file, we will typically also restart/reload the service so that it reads our modifications and applies those.

So far, so good. Now let's come back to our Ansible code. We are going to run this code in an automated fashion on a large number of servers, possibly hundreds. Considering this, it's not feasible for us to log in to each system to restart services after every change. This defeats the purpose of automating the process. Now, how do we ask Ansible to take action when an event occurs? That's where handlers can help.

You learned that Ansible modules are idempotent. They will enforce a change in state only if there is a configuration drift. When managing with Ansible, we will commit the preceding port change in the `default.conf` file inside `roles/nginx/files`. If we launch an Ansible run after making this change then, while executing, it will compare the file inside our role with the one on the system, detect the configuration drift, and copy it over to the changed file. With Ansible, this is where we will add a notification that will trigger a handler to run. In this case, we will call a handler to restart the Nginx service.

Let's now add this handler to `roles/nginx/handlers/main.yml`:

```
---
- name: restart nginx service
  service: name=nginx state=restarted
```

Handlers are similar to regular tasks. They specify a module's name, instance, and state. Why do we not add them with regular tasks then? Well, we only need to execute handlers,when an event occurs, not every time we run, ansible. And that's the exact reason why we create a separate section for it.

Now that we have written the handler, we also need to add a trigger for it. We will do this by adding the `notify` directive to `roles/tasks/nginx/configure.yml`, as follows:

```
---
 - name: create default site configurations
   copy: src=default.conf dest=/etc/nginx/conf.d/default.conf mode=0644
   notify:
     - restart nginx service
 - name: create home page for default site
   copy: src=index.html dest=/usr/share/nginx/html/index.html
```

 Even when multiple tasks notify the handler, it will be called only once, toward the end. This will avoid multiple restarts of the same service unnecessarily.

By now, our Nginx role layout looks more complete and has files, handlers, tasks, and directories with individual tasks to manage each phase of the Nginx setup. The role layout is as follows:

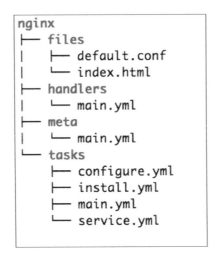

```
nginx
├── files
│   ├── default.conf
│   └── index.html
├── handlers
│   └── main.yml
├── meta
│   └── main.yml
└── tasks
    ├── configure.yml
    ├── install.yml
    ├── main.yml
    └── service.yml
```

Adding pre-tasks and post-tasks to playbooks

We would like to print status messages before and after we begin applying Nginx. Let's add it to our www.yml playbook with the pre_tasks and post_tasks parameters:

```
---
- hosts: www
  remote_user: vagrant
  sudo: yes
  pre_tasks:
     - shell: echo 'I":" Beginning to configure web server..'
  roles:
     - nginx
  post_tasks:
     - shell: echo 'I":" Done configuring nginx web server...'
```

In the preceding example, we only printed some messages using the echo command. However, we can create tasks using any of the modules available with Ansible, which can run before, or after, applying roles.

Running playbooks with roles

Let's now apply the refactored code to our hosts. We are going to launch only the site-wide playbook, that is, the site.yml file and then rely on the include statements and roles to do the magic:

```
$ ansible-playbook -i customhosts site.yml
```

Let's take a look at the following screenshot:

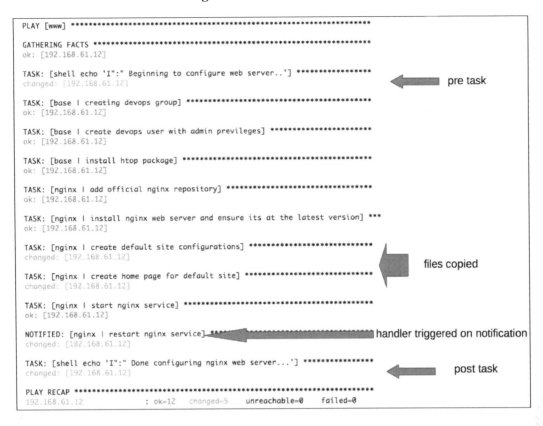

```
PLAY [www] ************************************************************

GATHERING FACTS ******************************************************
ok: [192.168.61.12]

TASK: [shell echo 'I":" Beginning to configure web server..'] *****************    <--- pre task
changed: [192.168.61.12]

TASK: [base | creating devops group] ********************************
ok: [192.168.61.12]

TASK: [base | create devops user with admin previleges] *************************
ok: [192.168.61.12]

TASK: [base | install htop package] ********************************
ok: [192.168.61.12]

TASK: [nginx | add official nginx repository] ********************************
ok: [192.168.61.12]

TASK: [nginx | install nginx web server and ensure its at the latest version] ***
ok: [192.168.61.12]

TASK: [nginx | create default site configurations] ********************************
changed: [192.168.61.12]                                                            <--- files copied

TASK: [nginx | create home page for default site] ********************************
changed: [192.168.61.12]

TASK: [nginx | start nginx service] ********************************
ok: [192.168.61.12]

NOTIFIED: [nginx | restart nginx service] *********************    handler triggered on notification
changed: [192.168.61.12]

TASK: [shell echo 'I":" Done configuring nginx web server...'] *****************    <--- post task
changed: [192.168.61.12]

PLAY RECAP ************************************************************
192.168.61.12              : ok=12   changed=5   unreachable=0   failed=0
```

In addition to the output we saw last time, there are some new messages this time. Let's analyze those:

- Before and after, roles are applied, pre-tasks and post-tasks get triggered; this prints messages using the shell module.

- We now have the code to copy to the config and .html file for our Nginx web server.

- We also see that the handler triggers an Nginx service restart. This is due to the change in the state for the configuration file, which triggers the handler.

Did you notice that tasks in the base role also get triggered, even when we have not mentioned the base role in the www playbook? This is where meta information is useful. Remember we had specified a dependency on the base role inside `meta/main.yml` for Nginx? That's what did the trick.

Dependencies:
```
- { role: base}
```

Review questions

Do you think you've understood the chapter well enough? Try answering the following questions to test your understanding:

1. Roles contain ___ and ___ subdirectories to specify variables/parameters.
2. How do you specify a dependency on another role?
3. When we add roles to a play, why is it not required that we use the `include` directives? How do the tasks, handlers, and so on, get added to the play automatically?
4. Why do we have a separate section for handlers if they resemble regular tasks?
5. Which module can be used to copy over static files to destination hosts?
6. How do you specify the tasks to be run before applying a role in a playbook?

Summary

In this chapter, you learned how to use roles to provide abstraction and to help modularizing code for reuse. That's exactly what you see community doing. Creating roles, and sharing them with you. You also learned about `include` directives, directory layout for roles, and adding role dependencies. We then went on to refactor our code and created a base role, the Nginx role. We also looked at how to manage events and take actions using handlers.

In the next chapter, we will extend the concepts of roles and start adding dynamic data with variables and templates.

3
Separating Code and Data – Variables, Facts, and Templates

In the previous chapter, we looked at how to write a role to provide modularity and abstraction. While doing so, we created the configuration file and copied the file over to the destination host using Ansible's copy module.

In this chapter, we will cover the following concepts:

- How do you separate data from code?
- What are Jinja2 templates? How are these created?
- What are variables? How and where are they used?
- What are system facts? How are they discovered?
- What are the different types of variables?
- What is a variable merge order? What are its precedence rules?

Static content explosion

Let's imagine that we are managing a cluster of hundreds of web servers spanning across multiple data centers. Since we have the `server_name` parameter hardcoded in to the `config` file, we will have to create one file per server. This also means that we will manage hundreds of static files, which will quickly get out of control. Our infrastructure is dynamic, and managing change is one of the most common aspects of a DevOps engineer's routine tasks. If tomorrow, our company policy states that we should run web servers on the port 8080 instead of the port 80, only in a production environment, imagine the headache you'd get having to change all these files individually. Wouldn't it be better to have a single file that takes dynamic inputs, which are specific to the host it's running on? This is exactly what templates are for and, as depicted in the following diagram, a single template could replace a multitude of static files:

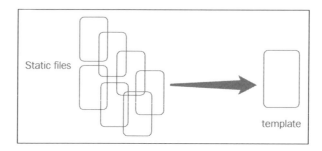

Before we define what a template is, let's begin by understanding how to separate code from data and how this would help us solve the problem of static content explosion.

Separating code and data

The real magic of infrastructure as code tools, such as Ansible, lies in its ability to separate data and code. In our example, the `default.conf` file is a configuration file that is specific to an Nginx web server. The configuration parameters, such as ports, users, paths, and so on, remain generic and constant at all times, no matter who installs and configures them. What is not constant are the values those parameters take. That's what is specific to our organization. So, for this, we would decide the following:

- Which port should Nginx run on?
- Which user should own the web server process?
- Where should the log files go?
- How many worker processes should be run?

Our organization-specific policies may also require us to pass different values to these parameters based on the environment or geography the hosts run in.

Ansible splits these in to two parts:

- The code that is generic
- The data that is specific to an organization

This has two advantages; one advantage is that it solves our problem of static data explosion. Now that we have separated the code and data, we can create `config` files flexibly and dynamically. The second advantage, you may realize, is now that the code and data are split, there is nothing in the code that is specific to a particular organization. This makes it easy to share the site with the world for anyone who finds it useful. That's exactly what you would find on Ansible-Galaxy or even on GitHub, fueling the growth of tools, such as Ansible. Instead of reinventing the wheel, you can download the code that someone else has written, customize it, fill in the data specific to the code, and get the work done.

Now, how is this code separate from the data? The answer is that Ansible has two primitives:

- Jinja templates (code)
- The variables (data)

The following diagram explains how the resulting file is generated from templates and variables:

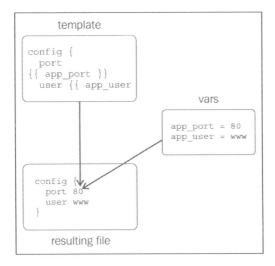

Templates provide placeholders in place of parameter values, which are then defined in variables. Variables can then be fed in from various places, including roles, playbooks, inventories, and even from the command line when you launch Ansible. Let's now understand templates and variables in detail.

Jinja2 templates

What is **Jinja** all about? **Jinja2** is a very popular and powerful Python-based template engine. Since Ansible is written in Python, it becomes the default choice for most users, just like other Python-based configuration management systems, such as **Fabric** and **SaltStack**. The name Jinja originated from the Japanese word for temple, which is similar in phonetics to the word template.

Some of the important features of Jinja2 are:

- It is fast and compiled just in time with the Python byte code
- It has an optional sandboxed environment
- It is easy to debug
- It supports template inheritance

The template formation

Templates look very similar to normal text-based files except for the occasional variables or code that surrounds the special tags. These get evaluated and are mostly replaced by values at runtime, creating a text file, which is then copied to the destination host. The following are the two types of tags that Jinja2 templates accept:

- `{{ }}` embeds variables inside a template and prints its value in the resulting file. This is the most common use of a template.

  For example:

  ```
  {{ nginx_port }}
  ```

- `{% %}` embeds statements of code inside a template, for example, for a loop, it embeds the if-else statements, which are evaluated at runtime but are not printed.

Facts and variables

Now that we have looked at the code that Jinja2 templates provide, let's understand where this data comes from, which is then embedded in the template at runtime. Data can come from either facts or variables. When it comes to a Jinja2 template, the same rules apply to the usage of facts and variables. Facts are a type of variable; the differentiating factor here is the origin of the two. Facts are automatically available and discovered at runtime, and variables are user-defined.

Automatic variables – facts

A lot of data in our systems is automatically discovered and made available to Ansible by the managed hosts during the handshake process. This data is very useful and tells us everything about that system, such as:

- The hostname, network interface, and IP address
- The system architecture
- The operating system
- The disk drives
- The processor used and amount of memory
- Whether it is a VM; if yes, is it a virtualization/cloud provider?

 Facts are collected at the very beginning of an Ansible run. Remember the line in the output that says **GATHERING FACTS *********? That's exactly when this happens.

You can find facts about any system by running the following command followed by a shortened output:

```
$ ansible -i customhosts www -m setup | less
    192.168.61.12 | success >> {
      "ansible_facts": {
        "ansible_all_ipv4_addresses": [
          "10.0.2.15",
          "192.168.61.12"
        ],
        "ansible_architecture": "i386",
        "ansible_bios_date": "12/01/2006",
        "ansible_cmdline": {
          "BOOT_IMAGE": "/vmlinuz-3.5.0-23-generic",
```

```
      "quiet": true,
      "ro": true,
      "root": "/dev/mapper/vagrant-root"
    },
    "ansible_distribution": "Ubuntu",
    "ansible_distribution_major_version": "12",
    "ansible_distribution_version": "12.04",
    "ansible_domain": "vm",
    "ansible_fqdn": "vagrant.vm",
    "ansible_hostname": "vagrant",
    "ansible_nodename": "vagrant",
    "ansible_os_family": "Debian",
    "ansible_pkg_mgr": "apt",
    "ansible_processor": [
      "GenuineIntel",
      "Intel(R) Core(TM) i5-3210M CPU @ 2.50GHz"
    ],
    "ansible_processor_cores": 1,
    "ansible_processor_count": 2,
    "ansible_processor_threads_per_core": 1,
    "ansible_processor_vcpus": 2,
    "ansible_product_name": "VirtualBox",
  }
}
```

The preceding output is in Ansible's own format and uses its core setup module. Akin to the setup module, there is another module by the name `facter`, which discovers and displays facts in the format discovered with Puppet, another configuration management system. The following is an example of how to use the `facter` module to discover facts for the same host:

```
$ ansible -i customhosts www -m facter | less
```

While using the `facter` module, a point that you need to note is that this module is not a core module and comes as part of extra modules. Extras modules are a subset of the Ansible module, which is used less frequently and is less popular in comparison with the core modules. Moreover, to use the `facter` module, you require the "`facter`" and "`ruby-json`" packages preinstalled on the target host.

User-defined variables

We looked at facts, which are automatically available, and the amount of data that is discovered is overwhelming. However, it does not provide us with every attribute of our infrastructure that we need. For example, Ansible can not discover:

- Which port we want our web server to listen to
- Which user should own a process
- Which system the users need to create, with which authorization rules

All this data is external to a system profile and is to be provided by us, the users. It's user-defined for sure, but how and where should we define it? That's what we are going to look at next.

Where to define a variable

Where a variable can be defined from is a complex phenomenon, as Ansible offers abundant choices in this regard. This also offers a lot of flexibility to users to configure portions of their infrastructures divergently. For example, all Linux hosts in a production environment should use local package repositories or web servers in staging and should run on the port 8080. All this without changing the code, and driven by data alone is done, by variables.

The following are the places from where Ansible accepts variables:

- The `default` directory inside a role
- Inventory variables
  - The `host_vars` and `group_vars` parameters defined in separate directories
  - The `host/group vars` parameter defined in an inventory file
- Variables in playbooks and role parameters
- The `vars` directory inside a role and variables defined inside a play
- Extra variables provided with the `-e` option at runtime

How to define a variable

After looking at where to define the variable from, we will start looking at how to define it at various places.

Here are some simple rules you can use to form a valid Ansible variable:

- A variable should always start with a letter

- It can contain:
  - ○ Letters
  - ○ Numbers
  - ○ Underscores

Let's take a look at the following table:

Valid variable	Invalid variable
app_port	app-port
userid_5	5userid
logdir	log.dir

We looked at the precedence rules and now we know that there are multiple places where you can define variables. Irrespective of the precedence levels, all use the same syntax to define a variable.

To define a simple variable in a key-value pair format, use, `var: value`, for example:

```
nginx_port: 80
```

A dictionary or hash can be defined as Nginx:

```
port: 80
user: www-data
```

An array could be defined as:

```
nginx_listners:
  - '127.0.0.1:80'
  - '192.168.4.5:80'
```

Templating the Nginx configurations

You have learnt a lot about facts, variables, and templates. Now, lets transform our Nginx role to be data driven. We will start templating the `default.conf` file for Nginx that we created earlier. The approach toward converting a file into a template would be as follows:

1. Create the directories required to hold templates and default variables inside a role:

   ```
   $ mkdir roles/nginx/templates
   $ mkdir roles/nginx/defaults
   ```

2. Always start with the actual configuration file, our end result of this process, to know all of the parameters it would take. Then, work backwards. For example, the configuration for the `default.conf` file on our system is as follows:

```
server {
        listen          80;
        server_name  localhost;
        location / {
            root    /usr/share/nginx/html;
            index  index.html;
        }
}
```

3. Identify the configuration parameters that you would like to generate dynamically, remove the values for those parameters, note them down separately, and replace them with template variables:

```
Template Snippets:
    listen {{ nginx_port }} ;
    root    {{ nginx_root }};
    index  {{ nginx_index }};

Variables:
    nginx_port: 80
    nginx_root: /usr/share/nginx/html
    nginx_index: index.html
```

4. If the values for any of the configuration parameters are supposed to be sourced from facts, typically system parameters or topology information, such as the hostname, IP address, and so on, then find out the relevant facts with the help of the following command:

   For example:

   `$ ansible -i customhosts www -m setup | less`

   To find out the hostname of the system:

   `$ ansible -i customhosts www -m setup | grep -i hostname`
```
    "ansible_hostname": "vagrant",
    "ohai_hostname": "vagrant",
```

5. Use the discovered fact inside the template instead of a user-defined variable. For example:

```
server_name   {{ ansible_hostname }},
```

6. Save the resulting file inside the template's directory, ideally with the `.j2` extension. For example, for `roles/nginx/templates/default.conf.j2`, the resulting file becomes:

```
#roles/nginx/templates/default.conf.j2
server {
    listen        {{ nginx_port }};
    server_name   {{ ansible_hostname }};

    location / {
        root    {{ nginx_root }};
        index   {{ nginx_index }};
    }
}
```

7. Create `roles/nginx/defaults/main.yml` and store the sane defaults as follows:

```
---
#file: roles/nginx/defaults/main.yml
nginx_port: 80
nginx_root: /usr/share/nginx/html
nginx_index: index.html
```

8. Once the template has been created, change the task in the `configure.yml` file to use the template instead of the copy module:

```
- name: create default site configurations
  copy: src=default.conf dest=/etc/nginx/conf.d/default.conf mode=0644
```

```
- name: create default site configurations
  template: src=default.conf.j2 dest=/etc/nginx/conf.d/default.conf mode=0644
```

9. Finally, it's time to remove the static file we used earlier with the copy module:

```
$ rm roles/nginx/files/default.conf
```

Then it's time to run the Ansible playbook:

```
$ ansible-playbook -i customhosts site.yml
```

Let's take a look at the following screenshot:

```
TASK: [nginx | create default site configurations] ****************************
changed: [192.168.61.12]

TASK: [nginx | create home page for default site]   ****************************  config file updated,
ok: [192.168.61.12]                                                                service notified

TASK: [nginx | start nginx service] ********************************************
ok: [192.168.61.12]

NOTIFIED: [nginx | restart nginx service]    **********************************
changed: [192.168.61.12]

TASK: [shell echo 'I":" Done configuring nginx web server...'] ***************
changed: [192.168.61.12]

PLAY RECAP *********************************************************************
192.168.61.12              : ok=12    changed=4    unreachable=0    failed=0
```

Let's analyze what happened during this run:

- We changed the configuration task to use the template instead of the copy module, which is reflected in the screenshot when a task shows its changed status
- Since the task has been updated, a notification gets triggered, which calls the handler to restart the service

Our code tree for the Nginx role looks like the following after we make this change:

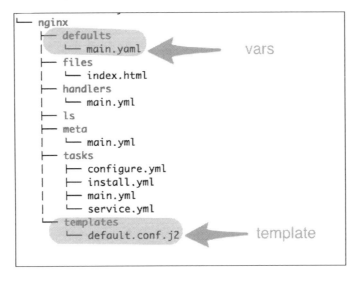

Adding another layer – the MySQL role

So far, we have been focusing on the single tier of our infrastructure, that is, the web server layer. Writing code for just one tier is not a lot of fun. Being a cool DevOps team, we will create a multi-tier infrastructure with database, web server, and then, a load balancer. We will start creating the MySQL role next, apply everything that we have learnt so far, and extend that knowledge with a few new concepts.

Here is our specification for the MySQL role:

- It should install the MySQL server package
- It should configure 'my.cnf', which is the main configuration for the MySQL server
- It should start the MySQL server daemon
- It should support Ubuntu 12.04 as well as CentOS/RedHat Enterprise 6.x

Creating the scaffolding for the roles with Ansible-Galaxy

So far, we have been doing all the hard work to understand and create the directory structure required by the roles. However, to make our lives easier, Ansible ships with a tool called **Ansible-Galaxy**, which should help us initialize a role by creating the scaffolding automatically and could help us follow the best practices. Ansible-Galaxy actually does more than that. It's a utility to connect to the repository of the freely available Ansible roles hosted at `http://galaxy.ansible.com`. This is similar to the way we use **CPAN** or **RubyGems**.

Let's start by initializing the MySQL role with Ansible-Galaxy using the following command:

```
$ ansible-galaxy init --init-path roles/ mysql
```

Here, the following is the analysis of the preceding command:

- `init`: This is the subcommand given to Ansible-Galaxy to create the scaffolding
- `--init-path` or `-p`: These provide the path to the roles directory, under which the directory structure is created
- `mysql`: This is the name of the role

Let's take a look at the following screenshot:

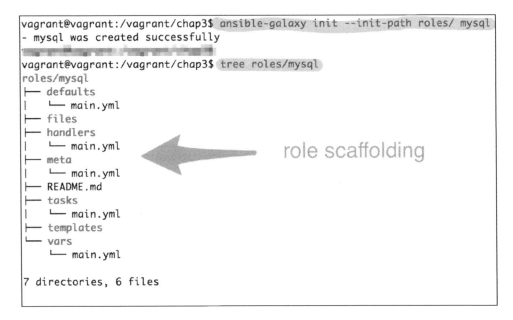

```
vagrant@vagrant:/vagrant/chap3$ ansible-galaxy init --init-path roles/ mysql
- mysql was created successfully

vagrant@vagrant:/vagrant/chap3$ tree roles/mysql
roles/mysql
├── defaults
│   └── main.yml
├── files
├── handlers
│   └── main.yml
├── meta
│   └── main.yml
├── README.md
├── tasks
│   └── main.yml
├── templates
└── vars
    └── main.yml

7 directories, 6 files
```

role scaffolding

The preceding diagram shows the directory layout created after you initialize the role with Ansible-Galaxy, which creates an empty role with a structure suitable for upload on to Galaxy. It also initializes the necessary components, including tasks, handlers, vars, and meta files with placeholders.

Adding metadata to the role

We used the meta file earlier to specify the dependency on another role. In addition to specifying the dependencies, meta files can specify much more data for the roles, such as:

- The author and company information
- The supported OS and platforms
- A brief description of what a role does
- The Ansible versions supported
- The category of software that this role attempts to automate
- The licensing information

Let's update all this data by editing `roles/meta/main.yml`:

```
---
galaxy_info:
  author: Gourav Shah
  description: MySQL Database Role
  company: PACKT
  min_ansible_version: 1.4
  platforms:
  - name: EL
    versions:
      - all
  - name: Ubuntu
    versions:
      - all
  categories:
  - database:sql
```

In the preceding snippet, we added metadata to the role, such as the author and company details, a brief description of what a role does, its compatibility with Ansible versions, the supported platforms, the category the role belongs to, and so on.

Using variables in tasks and handlers

You have learnt how to use variables in templates. That's not all the code there is used to define the variables. In addition to templates, we can also use variables inside tasks, plays, and so on. This time around, we have also committed to provide a multiplatform role, supporting Ubuntu and RedHat both. Unlike **Chef** and **Puppet**, Ansible uses OS-specific modules (for example, `apt` and `yum`) and not platform-independent resources (package). We will have to create OS-specific task files and call them selectively based on the OS they are going to run on. Here's how we do so:

- We will find a fact that will determine the OS platform/family. We have a couple of options here:
  - `ansible_distribution`
  - `ansible_os_family`

- RedHat, CentOS, and Amazon Linux are all based on `rpm` and have similar behavior. The same goes for Ubuntu and Debian operating systems, which are part of the same platform family. Hence, we choose to use the `ansible_os_family` fact, which will give us wider support.

- We will define variables from two places in the roles:
  - ○ From the default `vars` file with the sane defaults for Debian.
  - ○ From the variables specific to `os_family` if not Debian.
- We will also create OS-specific task files, since we may need to call different modules (`apt` versus `yum`) and additional tasks that are specific to that OS.
- For handlers and tasks, we will use variables to provide OS-specific names (for example, MySQL versus mysqld, for service).
- Finally, we will create the `main.yml` file, which will selectively include host-specific vars as well as task files by checking the value of this fact.

Creating variables

We will begin with the creation of variables. Let's set up the sane defaults for Debian/Ubuntu inside the `/mysql/defaults/main.yml` file:

```
---
#roles/mysql/defaults/main.yml
mysql_user: mysql
mysql_port: 3306
mysql_datadir: /var/lib/mysql
mysql_bind: 127.0.0.1
mysql_pkg: mysql-server
mysql_pid: /var/run/mysqld/mysqld.pid
mysql_socket: /var/run/mysqld/mysqld.sock
mysql_cnfpath: /etc/mysql/my.cnf
mysql_service: mysql
```

Then it will run on RedHat/CentOS machines, however, we will need to override a few of these variables to configure the RedHat-specific parameters.

 Note that the filename should match the exact name (RedHat) that is returned by the `ansible_os_family` fact with the correct case.

We will create and edit the `roles/mysql/vars/RedHat.yml` file, as follows:

```
---
# RedHat Specific Configs.
# roles/mysql/vars/RedHat.yml
mysql_socket: /var/lib/mysql/mysql.sock
mysql_cnfpath: /etc/my.cnf
mysql_service: mysqld
mysql_bind: 0.0.0.0
```

Finally, we will create the group_vars fact with one variable to override our default settings. You have learnt that you can specify variables in the inventory files, the group_vars and the host_vars facts. We will start using the group_vars fact for now. You could either create these in your inventory file or create a separate directory for it with the name group_vars. We are going to take the second approach, which is recommended:

```
# From our top level dir, which also holds site.yml
$ mkdir group_vars
$ touch group_vars/all
```

Edit the group_vars/all file and add the following line:

```
mysql_bind: "{{ ansible_eth0.ipv4.address }}"
```

Creating tasks

It's now time to create tasks. Following the best practices, we will split tasks into multiple files and use include statements, just like we did for Nginx. Let's start by creating the default main.yml file inside roles/mysql/tasks, as follows:

```
---
# This is main tasks file for mysql role
# filename: roles/mysql/tasks/main.yml
# Load vars specific to OS Family.
- include_vars: "{{ ansible_os_family }}.yml"
  when: ansible_os_family != 'Debian'

- include: install_RedHat.yml
  when: ansible_os_family == 'RedHat'

- include: install_Debian.yml
  when: ansible_os_family == 'Debian'

- include: configure.yml
- include: service.yml
```

We saw the include statements earlier. What's new here is the include_vars fact and the use of the ansible_os_family fact. If you notice:

- We are using the ansible_os_family fact here with the include_vars fact to determine whether to include OS-specific variables when the OS family is not Debian. Why not for the Debian system? That's because we are already specifying Debian-specific configurations in the default file. The include_vars fact works well with the preceding conditionals.

- We are also calling OS-specific installation scripts using the when condition. We have included two scripts for now to support the Debian and RedHat families. However, later on, we could just extend the scripts by adding more install_<os_family>.yml scripts to support additional platforms.

Now, let's create the install tasks for Debian and RedHat:

$ vim roles/mysql/tasks/install_Debian.yml

Then edit the file, as follows:

```
---
# filename: roles/mysql/tasks/install_Debian.yml
- name: install mysql server
  apt:
    name:"{{ mysql_pkg }}"
    update_cache:yes
```

$ vim roles/mysql/tasks/install_Redhat.yml

After running the preceding command, edit the file as follows:

```
---
# filename: roles/mysql/tasks/install_RedHat.yml
- name: install mysql server
  yum:
    name:"{{ mysql_pkg }}"
    update_cache:yes
```

In the preceding example, we used the apt and yum modules, respectively, for Debian- and RedHat-based systems. Following the best practices, we will write a data-driven role by providing the package name using a variable mysql_pkg. This variable is set based on the platform it runs on. Let's take a look at the following steps:

1. The next step is to create a task to configure MySQL. Since we know that every configuration file should be a template, we will create one for the my.cnf file, the default configuration file for the MySQL server:

   $ touch roles/mysql/templates/my.cnf.j2

   Then edit the file, as follows:

   ```
   # Notice:This file is being managed by Ansible
   # Any manual updates will be overwritten
   # filename: roles/mysql/templates/my.cnf.j2
   [mysqld]
   user = {{ mysql_user | default("mysql") }}
   pid-file      = {{ mysql_pid }}
   ```

```
socket = {{ mysql_socket }}
port = {{ mysql_port }}
datadir = {{ mysql_datadir }}
bind-address = {{ mysql_bind }}
```

2. We created a template with the `.j2` extension since it's a Jinja2 template. It's not a must, but a recommended practice.

3. All configuration parameters come from variables in the `{{var}}` format. This is a recommended practice for managing a configuration file. We could let the attribute precedence decide where the values comes from.

 It's good practice to add a notice to every file being managed by Ansible. This will avoid possible manual updates or ad hoc changes.

We will write a task that will manage this template, and copy over the resulting file to the desired path on the host:

```
---
# filename: roles/mysql/tasks/configure.yml
  - name: create mysql config
    template: src="my.cnf" dest="{{ mysql_cnfpath }}" mode=0644
    notify:
      - restart mysql service
```

We have a common configuration file template; however, the path to copy this varies from platform to platform, also based on the flavor of MySQL that you plan to use. Here, we are using a MySQL distribution that comes with the Ubuntu and CentOS repositories by default, and we will set the `mysql_cnfpath` path from the role variables, as follows:

*   On Ubuntu/Debian, use the command: `mysql_cnfpath = /etc/mysql/my.cnf`

*   On RedHat/CentOS, use the command: `mysql_cnfpath = /etc/my.cnf`

Also, we are sending the notification to the MySQL service restart handler. This will make sure that if there are any changes to the configuration file, the service will automatically be restarted.

To manage a service, we will create a service task and handler:

The task:

```
$ touch roles/mysql/tasks/service.yml
```

Then edit the file, as follows:

```
---
# filename: roles/mysql/tasks/service.yml
 - name: start mysql server
   service: name="{{ mysql_service }}" state=started
```

The handler:

```
$ touch roles/mysql/handlers/main.yml
```

After running the preceding commands, edit the file as follows:

```
---
# handlers file for mysql
# filename: roles/mysql/handlers/main.yml
 - name: restart mysql service
   service: name="{{ mysql_service }}" state=restarted
```

Here, the task and handler are similar to the Nginx service, so nothing much needs to be described. The only change is that we are using the `mysql_service` variable to decide the service name to start, or restart, the service.

Using variables in playbooks

Variables can also be specified in playbooks. The preferred method of doing so would be to pass them as role parameters, an example of which is shown as follows. This is typically useful when you have defaults in the role and you'd like to override some configuration parameters specific to your setup. That way, roles are still generic and sharable, and do not contain organization-specific data.

We are going to create a playbook to manage our databases and then we will include it in the site-wide playbook, as follows:

```
$ touch db.yml
```

Then edit the file, as follows:

```
---
# Playbook for Database Servers
# filename: db.yml
 - hosts: db
   remote_user: vagrant
   sudo: yes
   roles:
     - { role: mysql, mysql_bind: "{{ ansible_eth1.ipv4.address
     }}" }
```

Here, we assume that the host's inventory contains a host group by the name db. In our example, we have two db servers, one running on Ubuntu, the other running on CentOS. This is added as:

```
[db]
192.168.61.11 ansible_ssh_user=vagrant
ansible_ssh_private_key_file=/vagrant/insecure_private_key
192.168.61.14 ansible_ssh_user=vagrant
ansible_ssh_private_key_file=/vagrant/insecure_private_key
```

In the preceding playbook, we used a parameterized role, which overrides one variable, that is, mysql_bind. The value is set from a multilevel fact.

Let's take a look at the following screenshot:

```
roles:
    - { role: mysql, mysql_bind: "{{ ansible_eth1.ipv4.address }}" }
```
var in playbook : fact

parameterized role

A multilevel fact can also be specified as ansible_eth1["ipv4"]["address"] and both the formats are valid. Parameterized roles are also useful when we want to create multiple instances of the role, for example, virtual hosts and WordPress instances running on different ports.

Let's now include this playbook in the top-level site.yml file using the include statement:

Edit the site.yml file as follows:

```
---
# This is a sitewide playbook
# filename: site.yml
- include: www.yml
- include: db.yml
```

Applying a MySQL role to the DB servers

We are all set to configure our database servers. Let's go ahead and apply the newly created role to all the db servers we have in the inventory:

```
$ ansible-playbook -i customhosts site.yml
```

The following image contains the snippet of the output which is only relevant to the database play:

```
PLAY [db] ******************************************************************

GATHERING FACTS ************************************************************
ok: [192.168.61.11]
ok: [192.168.61.14]                      platform specific vars called

TASK: [mysql | include_vars {{ ansible_os_family }}.yml] *******************
skipping: [192.168.61.11]
ok: [192.168.61.14]

TASK: [mysql | install mysql server] **************************************
skipping: [192.168.61.11]
changed: [192.168.61.14]

TASK: [mysql | install mysql server] **************************************
skipping: [192.168.61.14]
changed: [192.168.61.11]

TASK: [mysql | create mysql config] ***************************************
changed: [192.168.61.11]                                    mysql
changed: [192.168.61.14]                                    setup

TASK: [mysql | start mysql server] ****************************************
ok: [192.168.61.11]
changed: [192.168.61.14]

NOTIFIED: [mysql | restart mysql service] *********************************
changed: [192.168.61.11]
changed: [192.168.61.14]

PLAY RECAP *****************************************************************
192.168.61.11          : ok=5    changed=3   unreachable=0    failed=0
192.168.61.12          : ok=11   changed=2   unreachable=0    failed=0
192.168.61.14          : ok=6    changed=4   unreachable=0    failed=0
```

We have explained the Ansible run in the previous chapters, when we created our first playbook as well as when we applied the Nginx role. The only new concept here is the include_var part. Ansible will check our condition based on the ansible_os_family fact and call variables specific to the OS. In our case, we have one Ubuntu and CentOS host each, and both of them call for the RedHat.yml file when it runs on the CentOS host alone.

What will be really interesting here is to find out what happened to our configuration files on each platform and which variables took precedence.

Variable precedence

We specified variable defaults, used them in inventory files, and defined the same variable from different places (for example, defaults, vars, and inventory). Let's now analyze the output of the templates to understand what happened with all those variables.

The following is the figure showing the `my.cnf` file on Ubuntu:

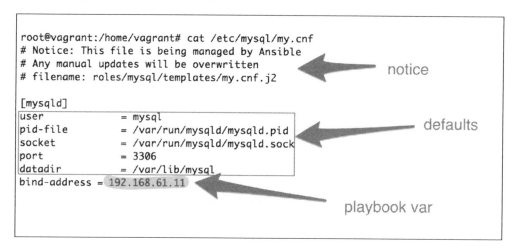

The following is the analysis of the screenshot:

- The file has a notice in the comments section. This can deter admins from making manual changes to the file.

- Most of the variables come from the defaults in a role. This is because Debian is our default family of operating systems and we already have sane defaults set for it. Similarly, for other operating system platforms, we are setting variable defaults from the `vars` directory in a role.

- Even though the `bind_address` parameter is specified in the defaults and `group_vars`, it takes a value from the playbook's role parameter, which has a higher precedence over the other two levels.

The following diagram explains what happens when there are variables defined at various levels. All of them are merged at runtime. If the same variables are defined in more than one place, the precedence rules apply:

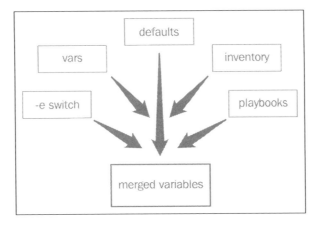

To understand the precedence rules, let's look at what happened on our CentOS host. The following is the my.cnf file created on CentOS:

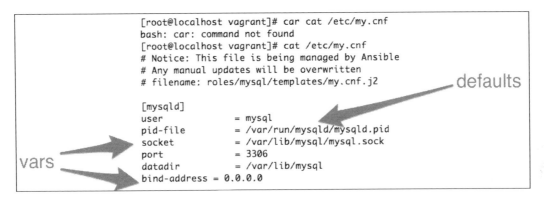

As seen in the preceding figure, in the case of CentOS, we see some interesting results:

- The values for **user**, **pid**, **datadir**, and **port** come from the defaults. We have looked at the merge order. If the variables are not identical, they are merged to create the final configuration.

- The value for a socket comes from vars as that's the only place it has been defined. Nevertheless, we want this socket to be constant for the RedHat-based system, hence, we specified it in the vars directory of the role.

- The `bind_address` parameter comes from the vars directory again. This is interesting as we have the `mysql_bind` variable defined at the following locations:
  - `Default` in a role
  - `group_vars`
  - `playbook`
  - `vars` in a role

The following figure depicts the precedence rules when we define the same variable more than once:

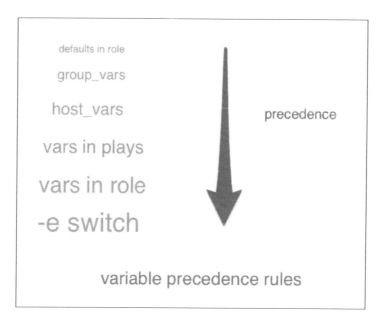

Since our role defines the `bind_address` parameter in the `vars` directory, it takes precedence over the rest.

There is a way to override a role parameter using extra variables or the `-e` switch while running Ansible. This is the supreme level of precedence for a variable that Ansible manages.

For example:

```
ansible-playbook -i customhosts db.yml   -e mysql_bind=127.0.0.1
```

In the preceding launch command, we used the `-e` switch, which will override all the other variable levels and make sure that the MySQL server is bound to `127.0.0.1`.

The best practices for variable usage

Overwhelming, eh? Do not worry. We will give you the recommendations on the best practices while using variables:

- Start with defaults in a role. This has the lowest precedence of all. This is also a good place to provide the sane defaults of your application, which can be later overridden from various places.

- Group variables are very useful. A lot of the time we will do region-specific or environment-specific configurations. We would also apply certain roles to a certain group of servers, for example, for all web servers in Asia, we apply the Nginx role. There is also a default group by the name "all", which will contain all the hosts for all groups. It's a good practice to put the variables common for all groups in "all" (`group_vars/all`), which can then be overridden by more specific groups.

- If there are host-specific exceptions, use `hosts_vars`, for example, `host_vars/specialhost.example.org`.

- If you would like to separate variables in different files, create directories named after the hosts and put the variable files inside it. All files inside those directories will be evaluated:

    ◦ `group_vars/asia/web`

    ◦ `host_vars/specialhost/nginx`

    ◦ `host_vars/specialhost/mysql`

- If you would like to keep your roles generic and sharable, use defaults in the roles and then specify organization-specific variables from playbooks. These can be specified as role parameters.

- If you would like role variables to always take precedence over inventory variables and playbooks, specify them in the `vars` directory inside a role. This is useful for providing role constants for specific platforms.

- Finally, if you would like to override any of the preceding variables and provide some data during runtime, provide an extra variable with Ansible commands using the `-e` option.

By now, our tree for the MySQL role and DB playbook should look like the following figure:

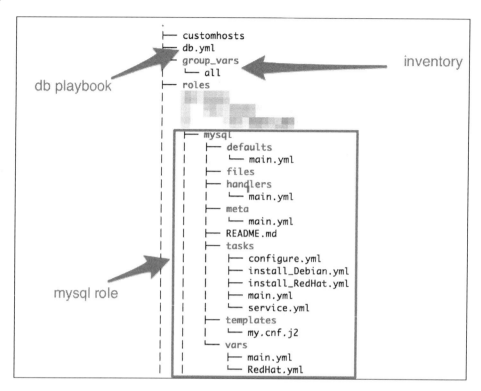

Review questions

Do you think you've understood the chapter well enough? Try answering the following questions to test your understanding:

1. How are Jinja2 templates different from static files?

2. What are facts? How are they discovered?

3. What is the difference between {{ }} and {% %} in the context of Jinja2 templates?

4. Can you use a variable anywhere apart from templates? If yes, where?

5. If you define a variable foo in the vars directory in a role and the same variable in the hosts_var file, which of these will take precedence?

6. How do you write Ansible roles that are supported on multiple platforms?

7. Where can you specify the author and licensing information in a role?

8. How do you provide variables while launching an Ansible-playbook command?

9. Which command would you use to create a directory structure required by the roles automatically?

10. How do you override a variable specified in the `vars` directory of a role?

Summary

We started this chapter by learning about why and how to separate data from code using Ansible variables, facts, and Jinja2 templates. You learnt how to create data-driven roles by providing variables and facts in templates, tasks, handlers, and playbooks. Additionally, we created a new role for the database tier, which supports both the Debian and RedHat families of operating systems. You learnt what system facts are and how they are discovered and used. You learnt how variables can be specified from more than one place, how they are merged, and the precedence rules. Finally, you learnt about the best practices for using variables.

In the next chapter, we will work with custom commands and scripts, understand what registered variables are, and deploy a sample WordPress application using all this information.

4
Bringing In Your Code – Custom Commands and Scripts

Ansible comes with a wide variety of built-in modules that allow us to manage various system components, for example, users, packages, network, files, and services. Ansible's battery-included approach also provides the ability to integrate the components with cloud platforms, databases, and applications such as **Jira**, **Apache**, **IRC**, and **Nagios**, and so on. However, every now and then, we would find ourselves in a position where we may not find a module that exactly does the job for us. For example, installing a package from source involves downloading it, extracting a source tarball, followed by the make command, and finally, "make install". There is no single module that does this. There will also be times when we would like to bring in our existing scripts that we have spent nights creating and just have them invoked or scheduled with Ansible, for example, nightly backup scripts. Ansible's command modules would come to our rescue in such situations.

In this chapter, we are going to introduce you to:

- How to run custom commands and scripts
- Ansible command modules: raw, command, shell, and script
- How to control the idempotence of a command module
- Registered variables
- How to create a WordPress application

The command modules

Ansible has four modules that fall in to this category and provide us the options to choose from while running system commands or scripts. The four modules are:

- Raw
- Command
- Shell
- Script

We will start learning about these one at a time.

Using the raw module

Most Ansible modules require Python to be present on the target node. However, as the name suggests, a raw module provides a way to communicate with hosts over SSH to execute raw commands without getting Python involved. The use of this module will bypass the module subsystem of Ansible completely. This can come in really handy in certain special situations or cases. For example:

- For legacy systems running a Python version older than 2.6, Ansible requires the `Python-simplejson` package to be installed before you run playbooks. A raw module can be used to connect to the target host and install the prerequisite package before executing any Ansible code.

- In the case of network devices, such as routers, switches, and other embedded systems, Python may not be present at all. These devices can still be managed with Ansible simply using a raw module.

Apart from these exceptions, for all other cases, it is recommended that you use either command or shell modules, as they offer ways to control when, from where, and how the commands are run.

Let's take a look at the following given examples:

```
$ ansible -i customhosts all  -m raw -a "uptime"
[Output]
192.168.61.13 | success | rc=0 >>
 04:21:10 up 1 min,  1 user,  load average: 0.27, 0.10, 0.04
192.168.61.11 | success | rc=0 >>
 04:21:10 up 5 min,  1 user,  load average: 0.01, 0.07, 0.05
192.168.61.12 | success | rc=0 >>
 04:21:12 up  9:04,  1 user,  load average: 0.00, 0.01, 0.05
```

The preceding command connects to all the hosts in the inventory provided with `customhosts` using SSH, runs a raw command uptime, and returns the results. This would work even if the target host does not have Python installed. This is equivalent to writing a `for` loop to an ad hoc shell command on a group of hosts.

The same command can be converted to a task as:

```
- name: running a raw command
  raw: uptime
```

Using the command module

This is the most recommended module for executing commands on target nodes. This module takes the free-form command sequence and allows you to run any command that could be launched from a command-line interface. In addition to the command, we could optionally specify:

- Which directory to run the command from
- Which shell to use for execution
- When not to run the commands

Let's take a look at the following example:

```
- name: run a command on target node
  command: ls -ltr
  args:
    chdir: /etc
```

Here, a command module is called to run `ls -ltr` on the target hosts with an argument to change the directory to `/etc` before running the command.

In addition to writing it as a task, the command module can directly be invoked as:

```
$ ansible -i customhosts all  -m command -a "ls -ltr"
```

Using the shell module

This module is very similar to the command module we just learnt about. It takes a free-form command and optional parameters and executes them on the target node. However, there are subtle differences between shell modules and command modules, which are listed, as follows:

- Shell runs the command through the '/bin/sh' shell on the target host, which also means that any command that gets executed with this module has access to all the shell variables on that system

- Unlike the command module, shell also allows the usage of operators, such as redirects (`<`, `<<`, `>>` , `>`), pipes (`|`) , `&&`, and `||`

- Shell is less secure than a command module, as it can be affected by a shell environment on the remote host

Let's take a look at the following example:

```
- name: run a shell command on target node
  shell: ls -ltr | grep host >> /tmp/hostconfigs
  args:
    chdir: /etc
```

Similar to using the command module, the preceding task runs the command sequence with the shell module. However, in this case, it accepts operators such as | and >>, does filtering with `grep`, and redirects the results to a file.

Instead of specifying this task as part of the playbook, it can be run as an ad hoc command with Ansible as:

```
ansible -i customhosts all --sudo -m shell \
 -a "ls -ltr | grep host >> /tmp/hostconfigs2 \
chdir=/etc"
```

Here, you need to explicitly specify the `--sudo` option, as well as module options as arguments, such as `chdir=/etc` and the actual command sequence.

Using the script module

The command modules that we learnt about so far only allow the execution of some system commands on the remote host. There will be situations where we would have an existing script that needs to be copied to the remote hosts and then executed there. Using the shell or command modules, this could be achieved in the following two steps:

1. Use a copy module to transfer the script file to a remote host.
2. Then, use a command or shell module to execute the script transferred previously.

Ansible has a tailor-made module that solves this in a more efficient way. Using a script module instead of command or shell, we can copy and execute a script in one step.

For example, consider the following code snippet:

```
- name: run script sourced from inside a role
  script:  backup.sh
- name: run script sourced from a system path on target host
  script: /usr/local/bin/backup.sh
```

As shown in the preceding code snippet, a script can be sourced either from:

- An inside file directory of the role when invoking this module from a task inside a role as shown in the first example

- An absolute system path on the control host (this is the host that runs Ansible commands)

Just like all the other modules, a script can also be invoked as an ad hoc command, as follows:

```
$ ansible -i customhosts www --sudo -m script \
    -a "/usr/local/backup.sh"
```

Here, the `script` module is invoked only on hosts that are part of the www group in the inventory. This command will copy a script at `/usr/local/backup.sh` from the control host and run it on the target nodes; in this case, all hosts in the www group.

Deploying a WordPress application – a hands-on approach

In our first iteration, we already configured an Nginx web server and a MySQL database to host a simple web page. We will now configure a WordPress application on the web server to host news and blogs.

Scenario:
Following our success of launching a simple web page in iteration 1, the project management department has asked us to set up a WordPress application to serve news articles and blogs in iteration 2.

WordPress is a popular open source web publishing framework based on the LAMP platform, which is Linux, Apache, MySQL, and PHP. WordPress is a simple, yet flexible, open source application that powers a lot of blogs and dynamic websites. Running WordPress requires a web server, PHP, and MySQL database. We already have an Nginx web server and MySQL database configured. We will begin by installing and configuring WordPress by creating a role for it and then later on, we will configure PHP.

To create the role, we will use the Ansible-Galaxy tool that we learnt about in the previous chapter:

```
$ ansible-galaxy init --init-path roles/ wordpress
```

This will create the scaffolding required for the WordPress role. By now, we know that the core logic goes in to tasks and is supported by files, templates, handlers, and so on. We will begin by writing tasks to install and configure WordPress. First, we will create the main tasks file as follows:

```
---
# tasks file for wordpress
# filename: roles/wordpress/tasks/main.yml
  - include: install.yml
  - include: configure.yml
```

 We are following best practices and further modularizing tasks here. Instead of putting everything in the main.yml file, we will create a install.yml file and a configure.yml file and include them from the main file.

Installing WordPress

The installation process of WordPress will be handled from the install.yml file in the tasks directory. The process of installing WordPress typically involves:

1. Downloading the WordPress installation package from https://wordpress.org.

2. Extracting the installation package.

3. Moving the extracted directory inside the document's root directory of the web server.

We will start writing code for each of the preceding steps mentioned, as follows:

```
---
# filename: roles/wordpress/tasks/install.yml
  - name: download wordpress
    command: /usr/bin/wget -c https://wordpress.org/latest.tar.gz
    args:
      chdir: "{{ wp_srcdir }}"
      creates: "{{ wp_srcdir }}/latest.tar.gz"
    register: wp_download
```

We saw some new features in the preceding steps. Let's analyze this code:

- We are using a new style to write tasks. In addition to using key-value pairs for tasks, we could separate parameters and write them one parameter per line in the key-value format.

- To download the WordPress installer, we used the command module with the wget command. The command takes the executable sequence with additional arguments, which are chdir, and creates.

- Creates is a special option here. With this, we specified the path to the file where WordPress installer is being downloaded. We will look at how this is useful.

- We also registered the result of this module in a variable with the name wp_download, which we will use in subsequent tasks.

 It is recommended that you use the get_url module, which is built in to Ansible to download files using the HTTP/FTP protocol. Since we want to demonstrate the usage of command modules, we chose to use that instead of using the get_url module.

Let's now look at the new concepts that we introduced previously.

Controlling the idempotence of command modules

Ansible comes with a wide range of modules built in it. As we learnt in *Chapter 1, Blueprinting Your Infrastructure*, most of these modules are idempotent, and the logic to determine the configuration drift is built in to the module code.

However, command modules allow us to run shell commands that are not idempotent by nature. Since command modules have no way to determine the outcome of the task, it is expected that these modules are not idempotent by default. Ansible provides us with a few options to make these modules run conditionally and make them idempotent.

The following are the two parameters that determine whether a command is run or not:

- Creates
- Removes

Both accept filename as the value of the parameter. In the case of creates, the command will not run if the file exists. The removes command does the opposite.

The "creates" and "removes" options are applicable for all command modules except for raw.

Here are some guidelines on how to use `creates` and `removes` flags:

- If the command sequence or script that you are executing creates a file, provide that filename as a parameter value
- If the command sequence does not create a flag, make sure you incorporate the logic of creating a flag file in your command sequence or script

The registered variables

We looked at variables earlier. However, we have never registered one before. In the tasks that we wrote to download WordPress, we use the following option:

```
register: wp_download
```

This option stores the result of the task in a variable by the name `wp_download`. This registered result can then be accessed later. The following are some of the important components of a registered variable:

- `changed`: This shows the status of whether the state was changed
- `cmd`: Through this, the command sequence is launched
- `rc`: This refers to the return code
- `stdout`: This is the output of the command
- `stdout_lines`: This is the output line by line
- `stderr`: These state the errors, if any

These can then be accessed as `wp_download.rc`, `wp_download.stdout` and could be used inside a template, in an action line, or more commonly, with the `when` statements. In this case, we are going to use the return code of `wp_download` to decide whether to extract the package or not. This makes sense because there is no point in extracting a file that does not even exist.

Extracting WordPress with a shell module

Let's now write a task to extract the WordPress installer and move it to the desired location. Before this, we also need to make sure that the document `root` directory has been created before running this code:

```
# filename: roles/wordpress/tasks/install.yml
- name: create nginx docroot
  file:
```

```
      path: "{{ wp_docroot }}"
      state: directory
      owner: "{{ wp_user }}"
      group: "{{ wp_group }}"

  - name: extract wordpress
    shell: "tar xzf latest.tar.gz && mv wordpress {{ wp_docroot
    }}/{{ wp_sitedir }}"
    args:
      chdir: "{{ wp_srcdir }}"
      creates: "{{ wp_docroot }}/{{ wp_sitedir }}"
    when: wp_download.rc == 0
```

Let's now analyze what we just wrote:

- We use the `file` module to create the document root directory for a web server. Parameters such as path, user, and group all come from variables.

- To extract WordPress, we use the `shell` module instead of a command. This is because we are combining the two commands with the `&&` operator here, which the command module does not support.

- We use the `when` statement to decide whether to run extract commands or not. To check the condition, we use the return code of the download command that we stored in the registered variable `wp_download` earlier.

Configuring WordPress

After downloading and extracting WordPress, the next step is to configure it. The main configuration for WordPress is inside `wp-config.php` under the `wordpress` directory that we extracted. As a good practice, we will use a template to manage this configuration file. The following is the code to configure WordPress:

```
---
# filename: roles/wordpress/tasks/configure.yml
  - name: change permissions for wordpress site
    file:
      path: "{{ wp_docroot }}/{{ wp_sitedir }}"
      state: directory
      owner: "{{ wp_user }}"
      group: "{{ wp_group }}"
      recurse: true

  - name: get unique salt for wordpress
    local_action: command curl https://api.wordpress.org/secret-
    key/1.1/salt
```

```
        register: wp_salt

    - name: copy wordpress template
      template:
        src: wp-config.php.j2
        dest: "{{ wp_docroot }}/{{ wp_sitedir }}/wp-config.php"
        mode: 0644
```

Let's analyze this code:

- The first task sets permissions for all WordPress files recursively.
- The second task runs a command locally and registers the results in the wp_salt variable. This is to provide WordPress with secret keys for additional security. This variable will be used inside a template this time.
- The final task is to generate a Jinja2 template and copy it over to the target host as the wp-config.php file.

Let's also look at the Jinja2 template:

```
# filename: roles/wordpress/templates/wp-config.php.j2
<?php
define('DB_NAME', 'wp_dbname');
define('DB_USER', 'wp_dbuser');
define('DB_PASSWORD', '{{ wp_dbpass }}');
define('DB_HOST', '{{ wp_dbhost }}');
define('DB_CHARSET', 'utf8');
define('DB_COLLATE', '');
{{ wp_salt.stdout }}
$table_prefix  = 'wp_';
define('WP_DEBUG', false);
if ( !defined('ABSPATH') )
    define('ABSPATH', dirname(__FILE__) . '/');
require_once(ABSPATH . 'wp-settings.php');
```

Here, we are filling in the values of the configuration parameters from variables. What is also interesting is that we are embedding the output of the salt download using the stdout variables:

```
        {{ wp_salt.stdout }}
```

The resulting file that is created from this template after filling in the variables and the `stdut` from a registered variable will be as follows:

```php
<?php
define('DB_NAME', 'wp_dbname');
define('DB_USER', 'wp_dbuser');
define('DB_PASSWORD', 'supersecure1234');
define('DB_HOST', '192.168.61.11');
define('DB_CHARSET', 'utf8');
define('DB_COLLATE', '');
define('AUTH_KEY',         'JM/U/vJz+Xg+8}-Z?svm:TF$!7+HOe#{ kKlUubJn$H*#bda' 8&XFC+-Nd&8iVXQ');
define('SECURE_AUTH_KEY',  'N1>A|awSX|H[I.Ts?Jrw:lQV_S3=dQaip+u8{(`P9w_uT-   0yqfP*6a#UF#{C,');
define('LOGGED_IN_KEY',    'U[Axce+vq`wCXr_G~hfzF~ >CeVgg*Gcf-Fnm$8w4!o2vuA .a0.~iRHZud&U)0<');
define('NONCE_KEY',        'WZ_0-lJzFKO]^6E[&-F| jN,=0]}3%,2b4`IW{qf_1~aL_Y!{;k~j9=gR_U1|+6S');
define('AUTH_SALT',        '9;B?)em?N(Eer$wcCt|ws.H]Z,Qwj%|w(7^@LYW+r[Z}i.5W--vC(16NX;6-N,yz');
define('SECURE_AUTH_SALT', 'o2sKrmOXvHJ?Nsz$uc,K6~QHfY8gHW&WT$S)H}S*PsMxIw:f-Z5|wr[k{v;K!ypT');
define('LOGGED_IN_SALT',   '|5XkSm+IpG5|9tOL]F|>}/QKg&-72Y48h+~anvU6xM9c^([^8-y}nc7dI4(tHp$i');
define('NONCE_SALT',       'm8+u~q=@K$o5v|]8]J1q_,21{?91@c+7oR:45[dQxOvhf(0}(g:yVTd)a$1x[(bV');
$table_prefix  = 'wp_';
define('WP_DEBUG', false);
if ( !defined('ABSPATH') )
        define('ABSPATH', dirname(__FILE__) . '/');
require_once(ABSPATH . 'wp-settings.php');
```

We will now add this new role to the `www.yml` playbook, so that it gets executed on all our web servers:

```
#filename: www.yml
  roles:
      - nginx
      - wordpress
```

Then, we will run the Ansible playbook only for web servers as:

```
$ ansible-playbook www.yml   -i customhosts
```

This will download, extract, and configure WordPress on all web server hosts. We still have not installed PHP and configured Nginx to serve WordPress pages, so our changes won't be reflected as yet.

Review questions

Do you think you've understood the chapter well enough? Try answering the following questions to test your understanding:

1. Why do we need command modules when Ansible has a battery-included approach?

2. When and why do we use the raw module?

3. How do we use the `creates` parameter with a shell when the command being executed does not create a file?

4. How are `command` and `shell` modules different? When would you use a shell?

5. If `var3` is a registered variable, how would you print its output in a template?

Summary

In this chapter, you learnt about how to run custom commands and scripts using Ansible's command modules, that is, raw, command, shell, and script. You also learnt how to control the idempotence of command modules using the `creates` and `removes` flags. We started using registered variables to store the result of a task that can then be used later to conditionally run other tasks or embed output in a template. Finally, we created a role to install and configure a WordPress application.

In the next chapter, we are going to start learning about how to control execution flow using conditionals, how to apply roles selectively, and also how to use conditional control structures in templates.

5
Controlling Execution Flow – Conditionals

Control structures refer to anything and everything that have an effect on a program's execution flow. Control structures are mainly of the following two types:

- Conditional
- Iterative

At times, we need to execute code conditionally based on a value of a variable, type of platform, or even a result of some other command. There are times when we also need to iterate multiple objects, such as list hashes or multilevel variables.

Most programming languages and tools use powerful but machine-friendly constructs, such as `if else`, `for`, `unless`, `do while`, and so on. However, Ansible stays true to its design tenet of being a human-friendly automation language and manages to achieve the same with the omnipotent `when` and `with_*` constructs, which are closer to the English language. Let's begin to explore how it does so.

In this chapter, we are going to cover the following topics:

- Using conditional controls with the `when` statements
- Using variables and facts to skip subroutines
- Applying roles selectively
- The conditional control structures in Jinja2 templates

The conditional control structure

Conditional control structures allow Ansible to follow an alternate path, skip a task, or select a specific file to import based on certain conditions. In a generic programming language, this is done with the help of `if-then`, `else if`, `else`, `case` statements. Ansible does this using the "`when`" statement. Some example conditions are:

- Whether a certain variable is defined
- Whether an earlier command sequence is successful
- Whether the task has run before
- Whether a platform on a target node matches the supported platforms
- Whether a certain file exists

The when statements

We have already used the `when` statement to extract the WordPress archive based on the result of another command, which is:

```
- name: download wordpress
    register: wp_download
- name: extract wordpress
    when: wp_download.rc == 0
```

This would be vaguely equivalent to writing a shell snippet, as follows:

```
DOWNLOAD_WORDPRESS
var=`echo $?
if [$var -eq 0]
then
    EXTRACT_WORDPRESS()
fi
```

In addition to checking the preceding code, we could simply write conditions based on the result of the task itself, as follows:

```
- name: extract wordpress
    when: wp_download|success
- name: notify devops engineers
    when: wp_download|failed
```

For the failed statement to work, we need to add the `ignore_errors: True` statement to the earlier task that registers the variable. The following flowchart depicts the same logic:

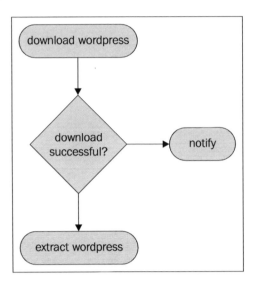

Fact-based selection

Facts are a good source of information to detect platform-specific information and make a choice based on it, especially when you have hybrid environments. Based on this selection, we could:

- Decide whether to execute a task
- Decide whether to include a task file
- Decide whether to import a file
- Decide whether to apply a role on the target node

We have already used fact-based selection while writing MySQL, where we used the fact `ansible_os_family` to:

1. Import the `vars` file for non-Debian-based systems.
2. Include platform-specific tasks for package installation.

The following code snippet shows both the use cases:

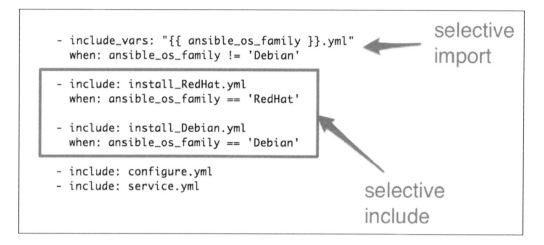

```
- include_vars: "{{ ansible_os_family }}.yml"
  when: ansible_os_family != 'Debian'

- include: install_RedHat.yml
  when: ansible_os_family == 'RedHat'

- include: install_Debian.yml
  when: ansible_os_family == 'Debian'

- include: configure.yml
- include: service.yml
```

selective import

selective include

Refactoring the MySQL role

Our existing MySQL role installs and configures only the server. More often than not, all we need to do is just install the MySQL client package and not the server. We don't have the ability to selectively do so.

The scenario:

We have been tasked to refactor the MySQL role and make it conditionally install the MySQL server based on a variable value. By default, it should just install MySQL client packages.

Boolean variables could be useful to set up an an on/off switch. We will add a variable and set its default value to `false`. This time, we will create a multilevel variable or a nested hash.

Multilevel variable dictionaries

So far, we have been naming variables as `mysql_bind`, `mysql_port`, and so on and using an underscore to categorize them. Variables can instead be better categorized and organized if you define them with multiple-level dictionaries, for example:

```
mysql:
  config:
    bind: 127.0.0.1
    port: 3306
```

Multilevel variables can then be accessed inside the code as `mysql['config']` `['bind']` or `mysql['config']['port']`. Let's now update the `roles/mysql/` `defaults/main.yml` file to use multilevel variables and also create a new Boolean variable `mysql.server`, which acts as a flag:

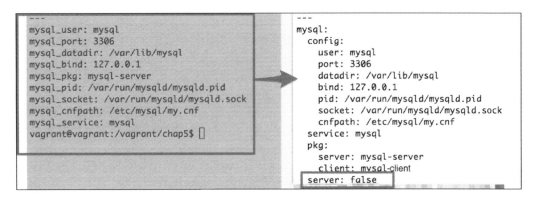

Additionally, we would have to update files in the `vars` directory in the `mysql` role to define the variables with a new style, all tasks, handlers, and templates to reference them appropriately. This process is added as part of the text to avoid redundancy.

Merging hashes

Multilevel variables or, in essence, dictionaries defined from different locations may need to be merged. For example, if we define default configuration parameters in the role `default` and then override a few from the `vars` directory in the role, the resultant variable `hash` should contain items from the **defaults** plus overridden values from **vars**.

Let's take a look at the following screenshot:

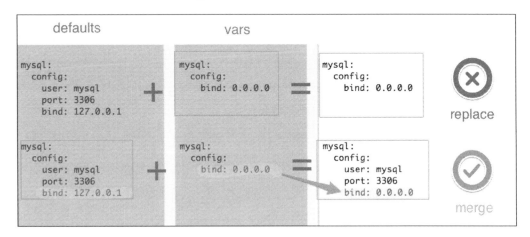

However, by default, Ansible will replace the dictionary, and in the preceding example, instead of getting a merged dictionary, we would lose the user and port vars as vars in the role has higher precedence. This can be avoided by setting the hash_behavior parameter to merge instead of replace, as follows:

```
# /etc/ansible/ansible.cfg
    hash_behaviour=merge
```

This should be set on the Ansible control host and does not require us to restart any service.

Configuring the MySQL server selectively

After refactoring the code and adding a flag controlled by a variable, we are ready to selectively configure the MySQL server. We have the mysql.server variable, which takes the Boolean value of True/False. This variable could be used to decide whether to skip server configurations, as follows:

```
#file: roles/mysql/tasks/main.yml
- include: configure.yml
  when: mysql.server

- include: service.yml
  when: mysql.server
```

Let's also add tasks to install the MySQL client package as well as the Python bindings required by Ansible's MySQL module:

```
---
# filename: roles/mysql/tasks/install_Debian.yml
  - name: install mysql client
    apt:
      name: "{{ mysql['pkg']['client'] }}"
      update_cache: yes

  - name: install mysql server
    apt:
      name: "{{ mysql['pkg']['server'] }}"
      update_cache: yes
    when: mysql.server

  - name: install mysql python binding
    apt:
      name: "{{ mysql['pkg']['python'] }}"
```

Here, the package names come from the following variable `hash`:

```
mysql:
pkg:
    server: mysql-server
    client: mysql-client
    python: python-mysqldb
```

By default, the `mysql.server` parameter has been set to `False`. How do we enable this only for the database servers? There are plenty of ways we can do so. We would choose playbook variables this time, since we have one dedicated to DB servers.

Let's take a look at the following screenshot:

```
---
# Playbook for Database Servers
# filename: db.yml
- hosts: db
  remote_user: vagrant
  sudo: yes
  roles:
      - { role: mysql }
  vars:
    mysql:
      server: true
      config:
        bind: "{{ ansible_eth1.ipv4.address }}"
```

Conditional control structure in Jinja2 templates

Ansible uses Jinja2 as a template engine. Hence, it would be useful for us to understand Jinja2 control structures in addition to the ones supported by Ansible tasks. Jinja2's syntax encloses the control structures inside the {%   %} blocks. For conditional control, Jinja2 uses the familiar `if` statements, which have the following syntax:

```
{% if condition %}
    do_some_thing
{% elif condition2 %}
    do_another_thing
{% else %}
    do_something_else
{% endif %}
```

Updating the MySQL template

The template that we created earlier to generate the my.cnf file assumes that all the variables referred in it are defined somewhere. There is a chance that this is not always the case, which could result in errors while running Ansible. Could we selectively include configuration parameters in the my.cnf file? The answer is yes. We could check whether a variable is defined and only then, we will add it to the file, as follows:

```
#filename: roles/mysql/template/my.cnf.j2
[mysqld]
user = {{ mysql['config']['user'] | default("mysql") }}
{% if mysql.config.pid is defined %}
pid-file = {{ mysql['config']['pid'] }}
{% endif %}
{% if mysql.config.socket is defined %}
socket = {{ mysql['config']['socket'] }}
{% endif %}
{% if mysql.config.port is defined %}
port = {{ mysql['config']['port'] }}
{% endif %}
{% if mysql.config.datadir is defined %}
datadir = {{ mysql['config']['datadir'] }}
{% endif %}
{% if mysql.config.bind is defined %}
bind-address = {{ mysql['config']['bind'] }}
{% endif %}
```

Let's analyze the preceding code:

- Since we are setting the default value for the mysql['config']['user'] parameter, there is no need to check whether it's defined. It's already handled gracefully.

- For all other parameters, we check whether the variable is defined using a condition, such as if mysql.config.pid is defined. This would skip the parameter if it's not defined rather than throwing an error.

Running a task only once

At times, a specific task in a role may need to be executed only once during a playbook execution, even though the role is applied to many hosts. This could be achieved with the run_once conditional:

```
name: initialize wordpress database
script: initialize_wp_database.sh
run_once: true
```

Since we are using the run_once option, the preceding task would run on the first host in the inventory that the role is being applied to. All consequent hosts would skip this task.

Executing roles conditionally

The Nginx role that we created earlier to set up web server supports only Debian-based systems. Running this logic on other systems could lead to failure. For example, the Nginx role uses the apt module to install packages, which would not work on RedHat-based systems, which depend on the yum package manager. This could be avoided by adding the when statement with a fact to selectively execute based on an OS family. The following is the snippet from the www.yml playbook:

```
#filename: www.yml (snippet)
- hosts: www
  roles:
    - { role: nginx, when: ansible_os_family == 'Debian' }
```

Review questions

Do you think you've understood the chapter well enough? Try answering the following questions to test your understanding:

1. What is the replacement for the if else statements in Ansible?
2. How can you selectively import platform-specific variables?
3. Why do Jinja2 templates use __ and __ to delimit control structures?
4. How would you skip running roles on incompatible platforms?

Summary

In this chapter, you learnt about how to control execution flow using the when statements, conditional imports, selective includes, and so on. You also learnt how to use variables and facts to selectively skip routines and execute platform-specific subroutines. We refactored the MySQL role to start using dictionaries of variables to conditionally configure the MySQL server and to use more intelligent templates with prechecks for defined variables.

In the next chapter, we will begin exploring the second type of control structures, that is. iterative control structures, where we will start looping arrays and hashes.

6
Iterative Control Structures – Loops

You learned about conditional controls in the previous chapter. Our journey into Ansible's world of control structures continues with iterative controls. Often, we need to create a list of directories, install a bunch of packages, or define and walk over nested hashes or dictionaries. Traditional programming languages use the `for` or `while` loops for iteration. Ansible replaces them with the `with` statements.

In this chapter, we are going to learn about:

- How to use iterative controls using the `with` statements
- How to loop arrays to create multiple objects at once
- How to define nested hashes and walk over them to create data-driven roles

The omnipotent with statement

Iterating plain lists, parsing dictionaries, looping a sequence of numbers, parsing through a path and selectively copying files, or just picking up a random item from a list could be achieved using the "Swiss knife" utility, `with` statement. The `with` statements take the following form:

```
with_xxx
```

Here, the xxx parameter is the type of data that needs to be looped, for example, items, dictionaries, and so on.

The following table lists the types of data that the `with` statement can iterate:

Construct	Data type	Description
`with_items`	Array	This is used to loop array items. For example, this is used to create a group of users, directories, or to install a list of packages.
`with_nested`	Nested loops	This is used to parse multidimensional arrays. For example, to create a list of MySQL users and grant them access to a group of databases.
`with_dict`	Hashes	This is used to parse a dictionary of key-value pairs and create virtual hosts.
`with_fileglobs`	Files with pattern match	This is used to parse a path and copy only those files that match a certain pattern.
`with_together`	Sets	This is used to join two arrays as a set and to loop over it.
`with_subelements`	Hash subelement	This is used to parse a subelement of a hash. For example, to walk over the list of SSH keys and distribute them to a user.
`with_sequence`	Integer sequence	This is used to loop a sequence of numbers.
`with_random_choice`	Random choice	This is used to pick up items from the array in a random order.
`with_indexed_items`	Array with index	This is an array with an index and is useful when an index for items is required.

Configuring WordPress requisites

While creating a role to install WordPress in *Chapter 4, Bringing In Your Code – Custom Commands and Scripts*, we created tasks to download, extract, and copy the WordPress application. However, that's not enough to launch WordPress, which has the following prerequisites:

- A web server
- PHP bindings for a web server
- The MySQL database and MySQL users

An Nginx web server and MySQL service have already been installed in our case. We still need to install and configure PHP along with the MySQL database and a user required for our WordPress application. To handle PHP requests, we choose to implement the PHP5-FPM handler, which is an alternative to the traditional FastCGI implementation.

The PHP5-FPM role

In **PHP5-FPM**, **FPM** stands for **FastCGI Process Manager**. PHP5-FPM comes with advanced features over **fastcgi**, which are useful for managing high-traffic sites. It is suitable for serving our fifanews site, which is expected to get a few million hits a day. Following our design tenet of creating a modular code, we would keep PHP functionality in its own role. Let's initialize the PHP5-FPM role using the Ansible-Galaxy command, as follows:

```
$ ansible-galaxy init --init-path roles/ php5-fpm
```

Defining an array

PHP installation will involve the installation of multiple packages, including php5-fpm, php5-mysql, and a few others. So far, we have been writing tasks one at a time. For example, let's take a look at the following code snippet:

```
- name: install php5-fpm
  apt: name: "php5-fpm"
- name: install php5-mysql
  apt: name: "php5-mysql"
```

However, this could become repetitive when we want to install multiple packages, also causing redundant code. Being committed to writing data-driven roles, we would drive the installation of packages through a variable, which takes a list of packages and then iterates the list. Let's begin defining the parameters required to list the packages, as follows:

```
---
#filename: roles/php5-fpm/defaults/main.yml
#defaults file for php5-fpm
php5:
  packages:
    - php5-fpm
    - php5-common
    - php5-curl
    - php5-mysql
    - php5-cli
    - php5-gd
```

```
        - php5-mcrypt
        - php5-suhosin
        - php5-memcache
      service:
        name: php5-fpm
```

Here is the analysis of the preceding code:

- The php5 variable is a variable dictionary, which would contain all the parameters that we pass to the php5-fpm role.

- The php5.packages parameter is an array of packages, one defined on each line in the code. This will be passed to a task that will iterate each item and install it.

- The php5.service parameter defines the name of the service, which would be referred to from the service task.

Looping an array

Let's now create tasks for the php5-fpm role. We need to install packages from the array and then start the service. We will split the package's functionalities in to two separate task files and call it from the main.yml file, as follows:

```
    ---
    #filename: roles/php5-fpm/tasks/main.yml
    # tasks file for php5-fpm
    - include_vars: "{{ ansible_os_family }}.yml"
      when: ansible_os_family != 'Debian'

    - include: install.yml
    - include: service.yml

    #filename: roles/php5-fpm/tasks/install.yml
      - name: install php5-fpm and family
        apt:
          name: "{{ item }}"
        with_items: php5.packages
        notify:
          - restart php5-fpm service

    #filename: roles/php5-fpm/tasks/service.yml
    # manage php5-fpm service
    - name: start php5-fpm service
      service:
        name: "{{ php5['service']['name'] }}"
        state: started
```

Along with tasks, the handler to restart the php5-fpm role can be written, as follows:

```
---
# filename: roles/php5-fpm/handlers/main.yml
# handlers file for php5-fpm
- name: restart php5-fpm service
  service: name="{{ php5['service']['name'] }}" state=restarted
```

Let's analyze the preceding code:

- **Main**: The main.yml file includes variables based on the ansible_os_family fact for non-Debian systems. This is useful for overriding variables that are platform-specific. After including the vars file, the main task goes on to include the install.yml and service.yml files.

- **Install**: The install.yml file is where we iterate an array of packages that were defined earlier. Since the file contains an array, we use the with.items construct with the php5.packages variable and pass the {{ item }} parameter as the name of the package to be installed. We could have alternatively passed the array directly, as follows:

  ```
  with_items:
    - php5-fpm
    - php5-mysql
  ```

- **Service and handler**: The service.yml file and the handler main.yml file manage the start and restart of the php5-fom service. It takes a dictionary variable php5['service']['name'] to determine the service name.

Creating MySQL databases and user accounts

WordPress is a content management system that requires a MySQL DB to be available to store data, such as posts, users, and so on. Additionally, it also requires a MySQL user with appropriate privileges to connect to the database from a WordPress application. We get one admin user while installing MySQL, however, it's a good practice to create an additional user account and grant privileges to the user as and when required.

Creating a hash

A **hash**, an abbreviation of hash table, is a dictionary of key-value pairs. It's a useful data structure to create a multilevel variable, which can then be programmatically to create multiple objects, each having their own values. We will define the databases and users as dictionary items in the `group_vars/all` file, as follows:

```
#filename: group_vars/all
mysql_bind:  "{{ ansible_eth0.ipv4.address }}"
mysql:
  databases:
    fifalive:
      state: present
    fifanews:
      state: present
  users:
    fifa:
      pass: supersecure1234
      host: '%'
      priv: '*.*:ALL'
      state: present
```

Here is the analysis of the preceding code:

- We defined this variable hash in the `group_vars/all` file instead of in the role. This is because we would like to keep roles generic and shareable, without adding data specific to our respective environments.

- We defined the databases and user configurations as multilevel dictionaries, or hashes.

Nested hashes

This multilevel hash is explained through the following diagram:

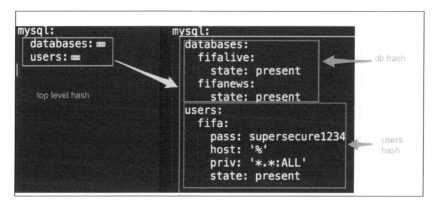

The following is the description of how this nested hash is structured:

- A MySQL variable is a hash with two keys: databases and users.
  For example:

```
mysql:
    databases: value
     users: value
```

- The values for each of these two keys are in turn hashes, or dictionaries of information, about the databases and users that are to be created. For example:

```
databases:
    fifalive: value
    fifanews: value
```

- Each database in turn is a dictionary of keys and values. For example, for the MySQL user `fifalive`, the key-value pairs are "state:present".

Iterating a hash

Creating databases and user accounts would typically require the creation of custom scripts with templates, which would then be called using command modules. Ansible instead comes with batteries, and staying true to this statement, it provides us with ready-made modules to perform MySQL-related tasks, that is, the `mysql_db` and `mysql_user` parameters. Using the `with_dict` statement, we will walk through the dictionaries of databases and users that we defined earlier, as follows:

```
# filename: roles/mysql/tasks/configure.yml
 - name: create mysql databases
    mysql_db:
      name: "{{ item.key }}"
      state: "{{ item.value.state }}"
    with_dict: "{{ mysql['databases'] }}"

 - name: create mysql users
    mysql_user:
      name: "{{ item.key }}"
      host: "{{ item.value.host }}"
      password: "{{ item.value.pass }}"
      priv: "{{ item.value.priv }}"
      state: "{{ item.value.state }}"
    with_dict: "{{ mysql['users'] }}"
```

Here is the analysis of the preceding code:

- The `mysql['databases']` and `mysql['users']` parameters are dictionaries that are passed to a task using the `with_dict` statements
- Each dictionary, or hash, has a key-value pair that is passed as the `{{ item.key }}` and `{{ item.value }}` parameters
- The `{{ item.value }}` parameter is a dictionary. Each key in this dictionary is then referred to as `{{ item.value.<key> }}`. For example, the `{{ item.value.state }}` parameter

The following diagram explains how this nested hash is parsed:

```
users:
  fifa:          item.key                    item.value.pass
    pass: supersecure1234
    host: '%'
    priv: '*.*:ALL'                          item.value
    state: present
```

Creating Nginx virtual hosts

After installing the `php5-fpm` manager and creating the MySQL databases and user accounts, the last bit of configuration that is left is to create a virtual host with Nginx to serve our WordPress application. The Nginx web server that we installed earlier serves a simple HTML page and is not aware of the existence of the WordPress application or how to serve it. Let's start by adding these configurations.

Defining the PHP site information

In addition to the `fifanews.com` site that we are setting up, we may also launch a few more sites related to soccer in future. Hence, we need to have the ability to programmatically add multiple sites with the same Nginx server. Creating a dictionary to define site information and embedding it into a template sounds like a good choice for this. Since site information is specific to us, we will add the variable hash to the `group_vars` file, as follows:

```
#filename: group_vars/all
nginx:
  phpsites:
    fifanews:
      name: fifanews.com
      port: 8080
      doc_root: /var/www/fifanews
```

We learned how to parse this dictionary from the Ansible task. Let's add a task that will allow us to walk through this dictionary, pass the values to templates, and create virtual host configurations:

```
#filename: roles/nginx/tasks/configure.yml
- name: create php virtual hosts
    template:
      src: php_vhost.j2
      dest: /etc/nginx/conf.d/{{ item.key }}.conf
    with_dict: "{{ nginx['phpsites'] }}"
    notify:
      - restart nginx service
```

Each item in this dictionary is passed to the template, in this case, to the php_vhost.j2 parameter. This in turn reads the hash and creates a virtual host template, which configures a PHP application, as follows:

```
#filename: roles/nginx/templates/php_vhost.j2
#{{ ansible_managed }}

server {
    listen {{ item.value.port }};

  location / {
    root {{ item.value.doc_root }};
    index index.php;
  }

  location ~ .php$ {
    fastcgi_split_path_info ^(.+\.php)(.*)$;
    fastcgi_pass    backend;
    fastcgi_index   index.php;
    fastcgi_param   SCRIPT_FILENAME   {{ item.value.doc_root
    }}$fastcgi_script_name;
    include fastcgi_params;
  }
}
upstream backend {
  server 127.0.0.1:9000;
}
```

Here is the analysis of the preceding code:

- The `{{ ansible_managed }}` parameter is a special variable that adds a comment notifying the server that this file is being managed by Ansible, with the path to this file in the Ansible repository, last modification time, and the user who modified it.

- The template gets a dictionary item and parses its values since it's a nested hash. This template has configuration for creating a php virtual hosts for Nginx using dictionary values set with `nginx.phpsites`.

- Configuration parameters provided with the dictionary include doc root, port, backend to use which make Nginx aware of how to handle incoming PHP requests, which backend to use, which port to listen on, and so on.

Finally, we add the new role to the `www.yaml` file, as follows:

```
# www.yml
roles:
     - { role: nginx, when: ansible_os_family == 'Debian' }
     - php5-fpm
     - wordpress
```

Run the playbook using the following command:

```
$ ansible-playbook -i customhosts site.yml
```

After the run is complete, it's time to test our work. Let's load the following URL in the browser:

```
http://<web_server_ip>:8080
```

Congratulations!! We've successfully created a WordPress PHP application with the Nginx web server and MySQL backend, fully configured. Now, we are ready to set up our fifanews site:

Welcome

Welcome to the famous five-minute WordPress installation process! Just fill in the information below and you'll be on your way to using the most extendable and powerful personal publishing platform in the world.

Information needed

Please provide the following information. Don't worry, you can always change these settings later.

Site Title	FIFA News
Username	admin
	Usernames can have only alphanumeric characters, spaces, underscores, hyphens, periods, and the @ symbol.

Password, twice

A password will be automatically generated for you if you leave this blank.

••••••••••••••• 🔑

••••••••••••••• 🔑

Strong

Hint: The password should be at least seven characters long. To make it stronger, use upper and lower case letters, numbers, and symbols like ! " ? $ % ^ &).

Your E-mail

admin@example.com

Double-check your email address before continuing.

Privacy

☐ Allow search engines to index this site.

[Install WordPress]

Review questions

Do you think you've understood this chapter well enough? Try answering the following questions to test your understanding:

1. Which statement in Ansible replaces the `for` loop?
2. How is the `with_____` statement used to iterate dictionaries?
3. How would you add a statement to a template that prints when, and by whom, it was modified?
4. How would you print the values of a nested hash?

Summary

In this chapter, you learned how to create multiple objects iteratively. We started with an overview of the omnipotent `with` statement and its various forms. Then, we dove deeper into iterating the two most essential data structures, which are, arrays and hashes. The `php5-fpm` role takes an array with a list of packages and creates a task to install those in a loop. To create MySQL databases and users, we defined variable dictionaries or hashes and iterated them. Finally, we added Nginx template configurations to create multiple virtual hosts serving PHP applications by iterating a nested dictionary.

In the next chapter, you will learn how to discover information about other nodes using magic variables.

7
Node Discovery and Clustering

For most real-world scenarios, we would need to create a cluster of compute nodes with the applications running on top, which are linked together. For example, the WordPress site that we have been building requires web servers and databases connected together.

Clustered infrastructure has a topology where one class of nodes should be able to discover information about the different, or the same, class of servers. For example, the WordPress application servers need to discover information about database servers, and load balancers need to know about the IP address/hostname of each web server that it's serving traffic to. This chapter focuses on what primitives Ansible offers to group together nodes and discover the attributes of interconnected nodes.

In this chapter, we will learn about:

- Discovering information about other nodes in the cluster
- Generating configurations dynamically using the magic variables discovered
- Why and how to enable fact caching

Node discovery with magic variables

We have looked at user-defined variables as well as system data, that is, facts. In addition to these, there are a few variables that define the meta information about the nodes, inventory, and plays, for example, which groups a node belongs to, what groups are part of the inventory, which nodes belong to which group, and so on. These variables, which are implicitly set, are called **magic** variables, and are very useful for discovering nodes and topology information. The following table lists the most useful magic variables, and their description:

Magic Variable	Description
hostvars	These are lookup variables or facts set on another host.
groups	This is the list of groups in the inventory. This can be used to walk over a group of nodes to discover its topology information.
group_names	This is the list of groups that the node belongs to.
inventory_hostname	This is the hostname set in the inventory file. It can be different to the ansible_hostname fact.
play_hosts	This is the list of all the hosts that belong to the current play.

In addition to the preceding table, there are a few additional magic variables, for example, the delegate_to, inventory_dir and inventory_file parameters, however, these are not relevant to node discovery and are less frequently used.

We are now going to create a new role to serve as a load balancer, which relies on this node discovery feature provided by the magic variables.

Creating the load balancer role

We created the Nginx and MySQL roles to serve the WordPress site. However, if we have to build a scalable site, we also need to add a load balancer to the mix. This load balancer will then act as an entry point for the incoming requests, and then spread the traffic across the available web servers. Let's consider the following scenario, where our fifanews site has become an instant hit. The traffic is growing exponentially, and the single web server approach that we have been using is showing cracks. We need to scale out horizontally and add more web servers. Once we start creating more web servers, we also need to have some mechanism to balance traffic across those. We have been tasked to create a haproxy role, which would discover all web servers in our cluster automatically and add to its configurations.

The following diagram explains this scenario with haproxy as a frontend, balancing the load across web servers in the backend. Haproxy is a widely used open source TCP/HTTP load balancer. Let's take a look at the following diagram:

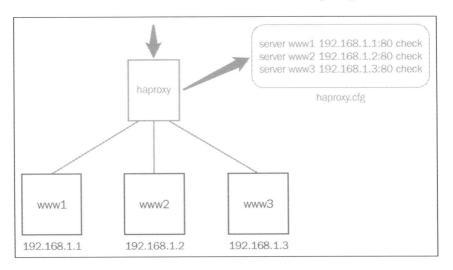

In the next steps, we will not only create a haproxy module, but also have it configured automatically with the IP addresses of all the web server nodes using magic variables:

1. Let's start by creating the scaffolding required to write this role, using the following command:

   ```
   $ ansible-galaxy init --init-path roles/ mysql
   ```

   The output will look as follows:

   ```
   haproxy was created successfully
   ```

2. We will now add some variables related to the haproxy role to the variable defaults:

   ```
   ---
   # filename: roles/haproxy/defaults/main.yml
   haproxy:
     config:
       cnfpath: /etc/haproxy/haproxy.cfg
       enabled: 1
       listen_address: 0.0.0.0
       listen_port: 8080
     service: haproxy
     pkg: haproxy
   ```

Even though it's a good practice to add a parameter for each configuration that haproxy supports, we will stick to a subset of parameters while writing this role; this is specially useful for node discovery.

3. Let's now create some tasks and handlers, which install, configure, and manage the haproxy service on an Ubuntu host:

```
---
# filename: roles/haproxy/tasks/main.yml
- include: install.yml
- include: configure.yml
- include: service.yml


---
# filename: roles/haproxy/tasks/install.yml
  - name: install haproxy
    apt:
      name: "{{ haproxy['pkg'] }}"


---
# filename: roles/haproxy/tasks/configure.yml
 - name: create haproxy config
   template: src="haproxy.cfg.j2" dest="{{
   haproxy['config']['cnfpath'] }}" mode=0644
   notify:
     - restart haproxy service

 - name: enable haproxy
   template: src="haproxy.default.j2"
   dest=/etc/default/haproxy mode=0644
   notify:
     - restart haproxy service


---
# filename: roles/haproxy/tasks/service.yml
 - name: start haproxy server
   service:
     name: "{{ haproxy['service'] }}"
     state: started


---
# filename: roles/haproxy/handlers/main.yml
- name: restart haproxy service
  service: name="{{ haproxy['service'] }}" state=restarted
```

Here is the analysis of the preceding code:

- As per the best practices, we created separate task files for each phase: install, configure, and service. We then called these from the main tasks file, that is, the `tasks/main.yml` file.

- The configuration file for haproxy will be created in `/etc/haproxy/haproxy.cfg` using a Jinja2 template. In addition to creating the configuration, we also need to enable the `haproxy` service in the `/etc/defaults/haproxy` file.

- Install, service, and handlers are similar to the roles that we created earlier, hence we will skip the description.

We have defined the usage of templates in the `configure.yml` file. Let's now create the templates:

```
#filename: roles/haproxy/templates/haproxy.default
ENABLED="{{ haproxy['config']['enabled'] }}"


#filename: roles/haproxy/templates/haproxy.cfg.j2
global
        log 127.0.0.1 local0
        log 127.0.0.1 local1 notice
        maxconn 4096
        user haproxy
        group haproxy
        daemon

defaults
        log global
        mode http
        option httplog
        option dontlognull
        retries 3
        option redispatch
        maxconn 2000
        contimeout 5000
        clitimeout 50000
        srvtimeout 50000

listen fifanews {{ haproxy['config']['listen_address'] }}:{{
haproxy['config']['listen_port'] }}
        cookie  SERVERID rewrite
        balance roundrobin
    {% for host in groups['www'] %}
```

```
       server {{ hostvars[host]['ansible_hostname'] }} {{
       hostvars[host]['ansible_eth1']['ipv4']['address'] }}:{{
       hostvars[host]['nginx']['phpsites']['fifanews']['port'] }}
       cookie {{ hostvars[host]['inventory_hostname'] }} check
   {% endfor %}
```

The second template that we created at `roles/haproxy/templates/haproxy.cfg.j2` is of particular interest to us pertaining to node discovery. The following diagram shows the relevant section with the usage of magic variables marked:

Let's analyze this template snippet:

- We are using the magic variable `groups` to discover all hosts that belong to the group www in the inventory, as follows:

  {% for host in groups['www'] -%}

- For each discovered host, we fetch facts as well as user-defined variables using the `hostvars` parameter, which is another magic variable. We are looking up facts and user-defined variables, as well as another magic variable, which is `inventory_hostname`, as follows:

  {{ hostvars[host]['ansible_eth1']['ipv4']['address'] }}

  ```
  {{ hostvars[host]['inventory_hostname'] }}
  {{ hostvars[host]['nginx']['phpsites']['fifanews']['port']
  }}
  ```

To apply this role to the load balancer host defined in the inventory, we need to create a play, which should be part of the `site.yml` file, which is our main playbook:

```
---
#filename: lb.yml
- hosts: lb
  remote_user: vagrant
```

```
    sudo: yes
    roles:
        - { role: haproxy, when: ansible_os_family == 'Debian' }


---
# This is a site wide playbook
# filename: site.yml
- include: db.yml
- include: www.yml
- include: lb.yml
```

Now, run the playbook using the following command:

$ ansible-playbook -i customhosts site.yml

The preceding run will install `haproxy` and create a configuration with all web servers added to the `haproxy.cfg` file in the backends section. An example of the `haprxy.cfg` file is as follows:

```
listen fifanews 0.0.0.0:8080
    cookie  SERVERID rewrite
    balance roundrobin
    server  vagrant 192.168.61.12:8080 cookie 192.168.61.12 check
```

Accessing facts for non-playbook hosts

In the earlier exercise, we launched the main playbook, which invokes all the other playbooks to configure the entire infrastructure. At times, we may just want to configure a portion of our infrastructure, in which case, we can just invoke the individual playbooks, such as `lb.yml`, `www.yml`, or `db.yml`. Let's try running the Ansible playbook just for the load balancers:

$ ansible-playbook -i customhosts lb.yml

Oops! It failed! Here is the snapshot of the snippet from the output:

```
TASK: [haproxy | create haproxy config] ****************************************
fatal: [192.168.61.13] => {'msg': "AnsibleUndefinedVariable: One or more undefined variables: 'dict object'
has no attribute 'ansible_eth1'", 'failed': True}
fatal: [192.168.61.13] => {'msg': "AnsibleUndefinedVariable: One or more undefined variables: 'dict object'
has no attribute 'ansible_eth1'", 'failed': True}

FATAL: all hosts have already failed -- aborting          FAILED

PLAY RECAP *********************************************************************
          to retry, use: --limit @/root/lb.retry

192.168.61.13               : ok=6     changed=0    unreachable=1    failed=0
```

Ansible exits with an error as it was not able to find a variable from the host, which is not part of the playbook anymore. Here is how Ansible behaves when it comes to magic variables:

- Ansible starts to gather facts while it runs the code on a host. These facts are then stored in the memory for the duration of the playbook run. This is the default behavior, and can be turned off.
- For host B to discover variables from host A, Ansible should have communicated with host A earlier in the playbook.

This behavior from Ansible can cause undesired results and can limit a host to discover information about nodes that are only part of its own play.

Facts caching with Redis

Failure to discover facts from non-playbook hosts can be avoided by caching facts. This feature was added in version 1.8 of Ansible and supports caching facts between playbook runs in **Redis**, a key-value in the memory data store. This requires two changes:

- Installing and starting the Redis service on the Ansible control node
- Configuring Ansible to send facts to the instance of Redis

Let's now install and start the Redis server using the following commands:

```
$ sudo apt-get install redis-server
$ sudo service redis-server start
$ apt-get install python-pip
$ pip install redis
```

This will install Redis on the Ubuntu host and start the service. If you have an rpm package-based system, you can install it as follows:

```
$ sudo yum install redis
$ sudo yum install python-pip
$ sudo service start redis
$ sudo pip install redis
```

 Before enabling facts caching, it's a good idea to first check if you are running a version of Ansible equal to, or greater, than 1.8. You can do so by running the command `$ ansible -version`.

Now that we have started Redis, it's time to configure Ansible. Let's edit the `ansible.cfg` file as follows:

```
# filename: /etc/ansible/ansible.cfg
# Comment  following lines
# gathering = smart
# fact_caching = memory
# Add  following lines
gathering = smart
fact_caching = redis
fact_caching_timeout = 86400
fact_caching_connection = localhost:6379:0
```

Let's now validate this setup by running the playbook, which configures web servers:

```
$ ansible-playbook -i customhosts www.yml
$ redis-cli
$ keys *
```

Let's take a look at the following screenshot:

```
redis 127.0.0.1:6379> keys *
1) "ansible_cache_keys"
2) "ansible_facts192.168.61.12"
```
facts cached in redis

Now we will try running the load balancer playbook again using the following command:

```
$ ansible-playbook -i customhosts lb.yml
```

This time it goes through successfully. It's able to discover facts for the web server, which is not part of the play.

Caching facts in files

Even though using Redis is the recommended approach, it's possible to cache facts in flat files as well. Ansible can write facts to files using the JSON format. To enable a JSON file as a format, we just need to edit the `ansible.cfg` file as follows:

```
# filename: /etc/ansible/ansible.cfg
fact_caching = jsonfile
fact_caching_connection = /tmp/cache
```

Ensure that the directory specified exists with the correct permissions:

```
$ mkdir /tmp/cache
$ chmod 777 /tmp/cache
```

After making these changes, all we have to do is run the playbook, and Ansible will start writing facts to JSON files named after the hosts created under this directory.

Review questions

Do you think you've understood the chapter well enough? Try answering the following questions to test your understanding:

1. Are magic variables different to facts? What are they used for?
2. Which magic variable would allow us to walk over a list of web servers and enumerate an IP address for each?
3. Why is facts caching required? What are the different modes for caching facts?
4. Will the `inventory_hostname` fact always be the same as the `ansible_hostname` fact?

Summary

In this chapter, you learned how to discover information about other nodes in the cluster to connect them together. We started with the introduction to magic variables and looked at the most commonly used ones. We then started creating a role for haproxy, which auto-discovers web servers and creates configurations dynamically. Finally, we looked at the issue of accessing information about hosts not in the playbook, and you learned how to solve it by enabling the caching of facts. Magic variables are very powerful, especially while orchestrating your infrastructure with Ansible, where discovering topology information automatically is very useful.

In the next chapter, you will learn how to securely pass data using vault, an encrypted data store.

8
Encrypting Data with Vault

Using variables, we saw how to separate data and code. Often, the data provided is sensitive, for example, user passwords, data base credentials, API keys, and other organization-specific information. Ansible-playbooks, being a source code, are most commonly stored in version control repositories such as a **git**, which makes it even more difficult to protect this sensitive information in a collaborative environment. Starting with version 1.5, Ansible provides a solution called **vault** to store and retrieve such sensitive information securely, using proven encryption technologies. The objective of using vault is to encrypt data that can then be stored and shared freely with a version control system, such as git, without the values being compromised.

In this chapter, we will learn about the following topics:

- Understanding the Ansible-vault
- Securing data using the Ansible-vault
- Encryption, decryption, and rekeying operations

Ansible-vault

Ansible provides a utility named Ansible-vault, which as the name suggests, lets you manage data securely. The Ansible-vault utility can either let you create an encrypted file by launching an editor interface, or encrypt an existing file. In either case, it will ask for a vault password, which is then used to encrypt the data with the AES cipher. The encrypted contents can be stored in a version control system without being compromised. Since the AES is based on shared secret, the same password needs to be provided for decryption too. To provide the password, there are two options, while launching Ansible, run the `--ask-vault-pass` option to prompt for the password, and the `--vault-password-file` option to provide the path to the file that contains the password.

Advanced Encryption Standard

Advanced Encryption Standard (AES) is an encryption standard based on the **Rijndael** symmetric block cipher, named after, and developed by, two Belgian cryptographers—Vincent Rijmen and Joan Daemen. Initially, established by (the U.S.) **National Institute of Standards and Technology (NIST)** in 2001, AES is an algorithm adopted by the U.S. government to share classified information, and is the most popular symmetric-key cryptography algorithm. AES is also the first publicly accessible open cypher approved by the **National Security Agency (NSA)**.

Being an open and popular standard, Ansible uses the AES cypher with a key size of 256 bits to encrypt data with the vault.

What to encrypt with the vault?

Ansible-vault can encrypt any structured data. Since YAML itself is a structured language, almost everything that you write for Ansible meets this criteria. The following are the pointers on what can be encrypted with the vault:

- Most commonly, we encrypt variables, which can be as follows:
    - Variable files in roles, for example, `vars` and `defaults`
    - Inventory variables, for example, `host_vars`, `group_vars`
    - Variables files included with `include_vars` or `vars_files`
    - Variable files passed to the Ansible-playbook with the `-e` option, for example, `-e @vars.yml` or `-e @vars.json`

- Since tasks and handlers are also JSON data, these can be encrypted with the vault. However, this should be rarely practiced. It's recommended that you encrypt variables and reference them in tasks and handlers instead.

The following are the pointers on what cannot be encrypted with the vault:

- Since the unit of encryption for the vault is a file, partial files or values cannot be encrypted. You can encrypt the complete file or none of it.

- Files and templates cannot be encrypted as they may not be similar to JSON or YML.

The following data are a good candidates for encryption:

- Credentials, for example, database passwords and application credentials
- API keys, for example, AWS access and secret keys
- SSL keys for web servers
- Private SSH keys for deployments

Using the Ansible-vault

The following table lists all the subcommands that the Ansible-vault utility comes with:

Subcommand	Description
create	This creates a encrypted file from scratch using the editor. This needs the editor environment variable set before launching the command.
edit	This edits the existing encrypted file with an editor, without decrypting the contents.
encrypt	This encrypts an existing file with structured data.
decrypt	This decrypts the file. Use this with care and do not commit the decrypted file to version control.
rekey	This changes the key or password used to encrypt or decrypt.

Encrypting the data

Let's perform some operations using Ansible-vault. We will start by creating an encrypted file. To create a new file from scratch, Ansible-vault uses the `create` subcommand. Before using this subcommand, it is important to set an editor in the environment, as follows:

```
# setting up vi as editor
$ export EDITOR=vi
# Generate a encrypted file
$ ansible-vault create aws_creds.yml
Vault password:
Confirm Vault password:
```

Launching this command opens up an editor specified with the editor environment variable. The following is an example of the `aws_creds.yml` file that you may create to store the AWS user credentials in the form of an access key and secret key. These keys are then used to make API calls to the Amazon web services cloud platform. Saving this file and exiting the editor will generate an encrypted file:

```
---
aws:
    access_key: AKIAJQYPXCXKOLOC4VFA
    secret_key: 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
```

aws security
credentials

You can check the type of file created and its contents by running following commands:

```
# Check file type and content
$ file aws_creds.yml
aws_creds.yml: ASCII text
$ cat aws_creds.yml
$ANSIBLE_VAULT;1.1;AES256
```

6461623666663623766303664356235383365653933313333316636636363623763633531323
4313134

3337303865323239623436646630336239653864356561640a36396639313531666163656
2333932

6132393231323038343331373564643862303261363562396664623230643338333532656
6343333

3136646536316261300a616438643463656263636237316136356163646616131336533623
9653434

3662613531313834393936363635353633738653062663635323865376234636234643761 3
4353863

3764663863623130346134356434323234383735666231626235653765306635646535343
2396436

3133666431366130663063653765356161616266653232316637653132356661343162396 33
1353863

3435663237396366323037386631396138643566346365656137346162383065626163656
4313464

37383465353665562383062336335316136303361306434393266343265366663538

Updating the encrypted data

To update the AWS keys added to the encrypted file, you can later use Ansible-vault's `edit` subcommand as follows:

```
$ ansible-vault edit aws_creds.yml
Vault password:
```

The `edit` command does the following operations:

1. Prompts for a password
2. Decrypts a file on the fly using the AES symmetric cypher
3. Opens the editor interface, which allows you to change the content of a file
4. Encrypts the file again after being saved

There is another way to update the content of the file. You can decrypt the file as follows:

```
$ ansible-vault decrypt aws_creds.yml
Vault password:
Decryption successful
```

Once updated, this file can then be encrypted again, as you learned earlier.

Rotating the encryption keys

As a good security practice, it's a good idea to change encryption keys used with Ansible-vault often. When this happens, it's essential to rekey all the files encrypted earlier using the vault. Ansible vault offers a `rekey` subcommand, which can be used as follows:

```
$ ansible-vault rekey aws_creds.yml
Vault password:
New Vault password:
Confirm New Vault password:
Rekey successful
```

It asks for the current password, and then allows you to specify and confirm your new password. Note that if you are managing this file with version control, you would also need to commit the change. Even though the actual contents are unchanged, rekeying the operation updates the resulting file that is created, which is part of our repository.

Encrypting the database credentials

Earlier while creating database users, we provided the passwords as plain text in `group_vars`. This can be a potential threat, especially when checked into a version control repository. Let's encrypt it. We will use the `encrypt` subcommand as we already have a variables file.

Since we are using the `group_vars` group to provide database credentials, we will encrypt the `group_vars/all` file as follows:

```
$ ansible-vault encrypt group_vars/all
Vault password:
Confirm Vault password:
Encryption successful
```

For encryption, Ansible-vault asks for a password or key to be entered by the user. Using this key, the vault encrypts the data and replaces the file with the encrypted content. The following diagram shows the plain text content on the left and the equivalent encrypted content on the right for the `group_vars/all` file:

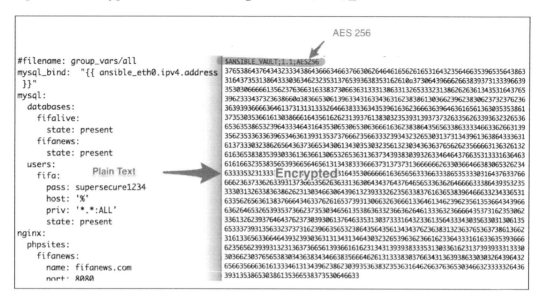

This file now can be safely checked into a version control system and shared. However, the following are the caveats users should be aware of:

- Unlike plain text, the resulting file is an encrypted format. It's not possible to get a different file format, for example, `git diff`, to compare the changes while committing to version control.

- It's not possible to use `grep`, `sed`, or any text search or manipulation programs on this file directly. The only way to do so is to decrypt it first, run the text manipulation utilities, and encrypt it back.

 Ensure that you use the same password for all the files that you are going to decrypt with one Ansible-playbook run. Ansible can take only one value for the password at a time, and will fail if the files in the same playbook are encrypted using different passwords.

Let's now run the Ansible playbook using the following command:

```
$ ansible-playbook -i customhosts site.yml
ERROR: A vault password must be specified to decrypt /vagrant/chap8/
group_vars/all
```

It fails with an error! That's because we are providing the playbook with encrypted data, without the key to decrypt it. The primary use for vault is to secure data while it's in the Ansible repository. Ultimately, these values need to be decrypted while running the playbook. The decryption password can be specified with the `--ask-vault-pass` option, as follows:

```
$ ansible-playbook -i customhosts site.yml --ask-vault-pass
```

This will prompt for "Vault Password" and then continue running Ansible code as usual.

Using a password file

Entering the password every time may not be ideal. Often at times you may also want to automate the process of launching Ansible playbook runs, in which case, an interactive way is not feasible. This can be avoided by storing the password in a file and providing the file to the Ansible playbook run. The password should be provided as a single line string in this file.

Let's create a password file and secure it with the correct permissions:

```
$ echo "password" > ~/.vault_pass
```

(replace password with your own secret)

```
$ chmod 600 ~/.vault_pass
```

> When the vault password is stored as plain text, anyone who has access to this file can decrypt the data. Make sure the password file is secured with appropriate permissions, and is not added to version control. If you decide to version control it, use **gpg** or equivalent measures.

Now this file can be provided to the Ansible playbook, as follows:

```
$ ansible-playbook -i customhosts site.yml --vault-password-file
~/.vault_pass
```

Adding the vault password file option to the Ansible configuration

With version 1.7, it's also possible to add the `vault_password_file` option to the `ansible.cfg` file in the defaults section.

Consider the following:

```
[defaults]
  vault_password_file = ~/.vault_pass
```

The preceding option gives you the freedom of not specifying the encryption password or the password file every time. Let's take a look at the following commands:

```
# launch ansible playbook run with encrypted data
# with vault_password_file option set in the config
$ ansible-playbook -i customhosts site.yml
$ ansible-vault encrypt roles/mysql/defaults/main.yml
Encryption successful
$ ansible-vault decrypt roles/mysql/defaults/main.yml
Decryption successful
```

Moreover, when starting with version 1.7, instead of storing a plain text password in the file, a script can also be provided in the `vault_password_file` option. When using the script, ensure that:

- The execute bit is enabled on the script
- Calling this script outputs a password on the standard output
- If the script prompts for user inputs, it can be sent to the standard error

Using encrypted data in templates

You learned earlier that since a template may not be a structured file such as YAML or JSON, it cannot be encrypted. However, there is a way to add encrypted data to the templates. Remember, templates are, after all, generated on the fly, and the dynamic content actually comes from variables, which can be encrypted. Let's discuss how to achieve this by adding SSL support for the Nginx web server.

Adding SSL support to Nginx

We have already set up an Nginx web server, now let's add SSL support to the default site by following these steps:

1. We begin by adding the variables, as follows:

   ```
   #file: roles/nginx/defaults/main.yml
   nginx_ssl: true
   nginx_port_ssl: 443
   nginx_ssl_path: /etc/nginx/ssl
   nginx_ssl_cert_file: nginx.crt
   nginx_ssl_key_file: nginx.key
   ```

2. Let's also create self-signed SSL certificates:

   ```
   $ openssl req -x509 -nodes -newkey rsa:2048 -keyout nginx.key -out
   nginx.crt
   ```

   The preceding command will generate two files, `nginx.key` and `nginx.crt`. These are the files that we will have copied over to the web server.

3. Let's add the contents of these files to the variables, and create the `group_vars/www` file:

   ```
   # file: group_vars/www
   ---
   nginx_ssl_cert_content: |
        -----BEGIN CERTIFICATE-----
        -----END CERTIFICATE-----
   nginx_ssl_key_content: |
        -----BEGIN PRIVATE KEY-----
        -----END PRIVATE KEY-----
   ```

   In the preceding example, we are just adding placeholders that are to be replaced with the actual contents for the key and certificate. These keys and certificates should not be exposed in a version control system.

4. Let's encrypt this file using the vault:

   ```
   $ ansible-vault encrypt group_vars/www
   Encryption successful
   ```

   Since we have already provided the path to the vault password in the configuration, the Ansible-vault does not ask for the password.

5. Let's now create the templates, which add these keys:

```
# filename: roles/nginx/templates/nginx.crt.j2
{{ nginx_ssl_cert_content }}


# filename: roles/nginx/templates/nginx.key.j2
{{ nginx_ssl_key_content }}
```

6. Also, let's add a virtual host `config` file to the SSL:

```
# filename: roles/nginx/templates/nginx.key.j2
server {
  listen {{ nginx_port_ssl }};
  server_name {{ ansible_hostname }};
  ssl on;
  ssl_certificate {{ nginx_ssl_path }}/{{
  nginx_ssl_cert_file }};
  ssl_certificate_key {{ nginx_ssl_path }}/{{
  nginx_ssl_key_file }};

  location / {
    root {{ nginx_root }};
    index {{ nginx_index }};
  }
}
```

7. We also need to create a task file to configure the SSL site, which will create the required directory, files, and configurations:

```
---
# filename: roles/nginx/tasks/configure_ssl.yml
 - name: create ssl directory
    file: path="{{ nginx_ssl_path }}" state=directory
    owner=root group=root
 - name: add ssl key
    template: src=nginx.key.j2 dest="{{ nginx_ssl_path
    }}/nginx.key" mode=0644
 - name: add ssl cert
    template: src=nginx.crt.j2 dest="{{ nginx_ssl_path
    }}/nginx.crt" mode=0644
 - name: create ssl site configurations
    template: src=default_ssl.conf.j2 dest="{{ nginx_ssl_path
    }}/default_ssl.conf" mode=0644
    notify:
    - restart nginx service
```

8. Finally, let's call this task selectively based on whether the `nginx_ssl var` parameter is set to true:

```
# filename: roles/nginx/tasks/main.yml
 - include: configure_ssl.yml
     when: nginx_ssl
```

9. Now, run the playbook as follows:

```
$ ansible-playbook -i customhosts  site.yml
```

This should configure the default SSL site running at port 443 with self-signed certificates. Now, you should be able to open the web server address with the `https` secure protocol as follows:

Of course, it should show a warning as our certificate is self-signed and not provided by a designated certification authority.

Review questions

Do you think you've understood the chapter well enough? Try answering the following questions to test your understanding:

1. Why is there a need to encrypt the data provided to Ansible playbooks?
2. What is AES, and what is a symmetric-key cipher?
3. What are the two methods to update a file previously encrypted with the vault?
4. What is the parameter that is added to the Ansible configuration file to make it aware of the location of the vault password file?

Summary

In this chapter, you learned how to secure the data passed to the playbooks using Ansible-vault. We started with the need to encrypt data, how the vault works, and which cipher it uses. We then started to dive into the Ansible-vault utility and basic operations such as creating encrypted files, decrypting, rekeying, and so on. You also learned how to encrypt existing files by running Ansible-vault on the `vars` file holding the database credentials. Finally, we added SSL support to Nginx and you learned how to securely store private keys and certificates for the web server using the vault and copying them using templates. Note that Ansible vault offers a way to provide data to Ansible modules securely. In addition to using the vault, additional system security measures are advised that do not come under the purview of this text.

After learning about vault, in the next chapter, we will start learning about the various approaches to managing multiple environments such as development, staging, and production with Ansible. These environments typically map to the software development workflow.

9
Managing Environments

Most organizations start with a single environment while building their infrastructures. However, as the complexity grows, it is imperative that we have a workflow that involves writing code and testing it in development environments, followed by an intensive QA cycle to make sure that the code is tested for stability in the staging, or preproduction, environment before we finally release it to production. In order to simulate a real-world behavior, these environments have to run identical stacks of applications, but most likely at different scales. For example, staging will be a small-scale replica of production with fewer servers, and most commonly, development environments would run on individual workstations in virtualized environments. Even though all these environments run an identical application stack, they have to be isolated from each other and must have environment-specific configurations, explained as follows:

- The applications in the `dev` group should not be pointing at databases in staging and vice versa
- A production environment may have its own package repository
- A staging environment may run a web server on port `8080`, whereas all other environments run it on port `80`

With roles, we could create a modular code to configure these environments identically for all environments. Another important property of Ansible is its ability to separate code from data. Using these two in combination, we could model the infrastructure in a way that we would be able to create environment-specific configurations without having to modify the roles. We would be able to create them just by providing the variables from different places. Let's take a look at the following screenshot:

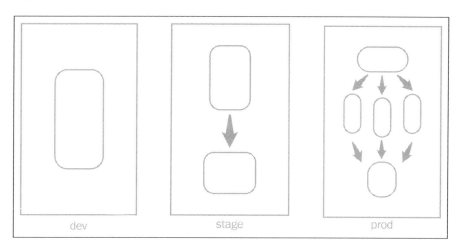

The preceding diagram portrays three different environments, which are dev, stage, and production, within the same organization. All three run the same application stack, which involves a load balancer, web servers, and database servers. However, the two things to note here are that:

- Each environment has a different scale based on which host can be configured to run one or more roles (for example, db plus www).
- Each environment is isolated from the other. A web server in a production environment will not connect to a database in staging, and vice versa.

In this chapter, we are going to cover the following topics:

- Managing multiple environments with Ansible
- Separating inventory files per environment
- Using the group_vars and host_vars groups to specify environment-specific configurations

Approaches for managing environments

You have already learned about the need to create different environments with identical roles, but with different data. At the time of writing this, more than one approach exists for managing such multiple environment scenarios with Ansible. We are going to discuss two approaches here, and you can use your best judgment to pick either of the two or create your own approach. There is no explicit way to create an environment, but the following are the built-in features of Ansible, which could come in handy:

- The use of an inventory to group together hosts that belong to one environment and isolate them from the hosts in other environments
- The use of inventory variables, such as the `group_vars` and `host_vars` groups, to provide environment-specific variables

Before we proceed, it would be useful to review the inventory groups, variables, and precedence rules that are applicable to them.

The inventory groups and variables

You have already learned learned that the Ansible inventory follows an INI style configuration, where hosts are grouped together with group tags enclosed in square brackets, as shown in the following figure:

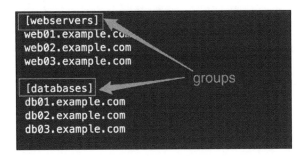

The inventory variables can then be specified so that they match these group names using `group_vars` or match specific hosts in the `host_vars` files. Apart from these group names, there is a provision to specify default variables for the `group_vars` and `host_vars` files using a file named "all", which gives rise to the following structure:

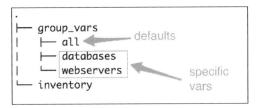

In such a case, if you specify the same variable in the `all` and `webserver` files, the one variable that is more specific will take precedence. What this means is, if you define a variable in 'all' and define it again in the 'webserver' group under `group_vars`, the value of the parameters will be set to the one defined in 'webserver', which is more specific. This is the behavior that we exploit in the approaches, which are as follows.

Approach 1 – using nested groups in an inventory

In addition to being able to create groups using the INI style, Ansible supports nested groups, where a complete group can be part of another parent group. The first approach is based on this feature and is discussed step by step, as follows:

1. Create an environment directory to store environment-specific inventory files. It's a good idea to name them after the environments. Add hosts that are specific to that environment and group them. A group can be of any criteria, such as a role, location, server racks, and so on. For example, create a 'webservers' group to add all the Apache web servers, or a group called 'in' to add all the hosts belonging to that location.

2. Add a parent group named after the environment name, such as, production, development, staging, and so on, and include all other groups that belong to that environment as a child. Each of these in turn include a group of hosts, for example:

```
[dev:children]
    webservers
    databases
```

3. Now, create the common/default group variables in the `group_vars/all` file. These variables then can be overridden from the environment-specific files.

4. To specify the environment-specific variables, create the `group_vars/` `{{env}}` file, which is shown as follows:

```
group_vars
    |_ all
    |_ dev
    |_ stage
```

This is also going to override the variables in the `all` group. The following diagram shows the file structure created with this approach:

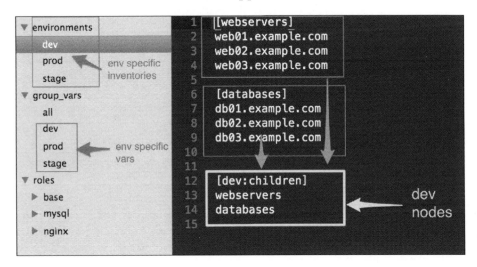

Once this has been created, it's just a matter of calling the environment-specific inventory with the `ansible-playbook` command run.

For example, let's take a look at the following command:

```
$ ansible-playbook -i environments/dev site.yml
```

Approach 2 – using environment-specific inventory variables

The second approach does not require nested groups and relies on the following two features of Ansible:

- The `-i` option of Ansible-playbook also accepts a directory that can contain one or more inventory files
- The `host` and `group` variables can be relative to the inventory files in addition to the `group_vars` and `host_vars` groups in the root of the Ansible repository

This approach will create completely isolated variable files for each environment. The file structure we created is portrayed in the following diagram:

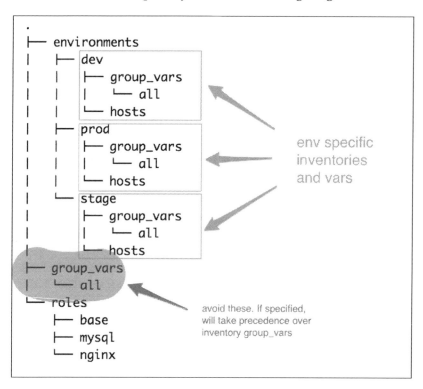

The following is the step-by-step method used for this approach:

1. Create an environment directory in the root of the Ansible repository. Under this, create one directory per environment.

2. Each of the environment directories contain two things:
   ◦ A host's inventory.
   ◦ Inventory variables, for example, group_vars and host_vars. To make environment-specific changes, group_vars is relevant to us.

3. Each environment contains its own group_vars directory, which in turn can have one or more files, including the all file as default. No two environments share these variables with others.

Caution: In addition to the environment-specific `group_vars` group, it's possible to use the `group_vars` file residing on top of the Ansible-playbook repository. However, it's recommended that you don't use it with this approach, as environment-specific changes are overridden by the values in the playbook `group_vars` if they are same.

With this approach, the playbook can be launched specific to an environment as:

```
$ ansible-playbook -i environments/dev site.py
```

Here, `environments/dev` is a directory.

Creating a development environment

After learning about how to manage environments, let's try it out by refactoring our existing code and create a dev environment. To test it, let's create a variable called "env_name" and change the default page of Nginx to dynamically use this variable and print the environment name. We will then try to override this variable from the environment. Let's take a look at the following steps:

1. Let's begin by setting the default variable:

   ```
   #group_vars/all
   env_name: default
   ```

2. Then, change the Nginx task to use a template instead of a static file, so make the following modification in the `roles/nginx/tasks/configure.yml` file:

   ```
   - name: create home page for default site
     copy: src=index.html
       dest=/usr/share/nginx/html/index.html
   ```

   Modify it into the following code:

   ```
   - name: create home page for default site
     template:
       src: index.html.j2
       dest: /usr/share/nginx/html/index.html
   ```

3. Let's now try running the playbook without creating the environment:

   ```
   $ ansible-playbook -i customhosts www.yml
   ```

4. After the run is complete, let's check the default web page:

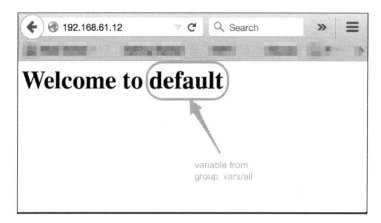

5. It prints the value of the variable that we set from the `group_vars/all` file, the default value.

6. Let's now create a file that would allow us to manage a `dev` environment. Since we are going to use the same set of hosts, we could just convert our existing inventory to dev and add a parent group after the name of the environment:

```
$ mkdir environments/

$ mv customhosts environments/dev

    [ edit   environments/dev ]
```

7. Add all the groups to the `dev` environment as:

```
[dev:children]
db
www
lb
```

The inventory file is shown as follows and we've to make the following changes:

1. Now, let's create a `group_vars` file for the `dev` environment and override the environment name:

```
#file: environments/dev
env_name: dev
```

2. This time, we are going to run the playbook as:

```
$ ansible-playbook -i environments/dev www.yml
```

We'll see the following screenshot as the output:

Review questions

Do you think you've understood this chapter well enough? Try answering the following questions to test your understanding:

1. How do you specify multiple host inventories for the same environment?
2. If you define a variable in the `environments/dev/group_vars/all` file and the same in the `group_vars/all` file, which one will take precedence?
3. How do you create a group of groups in a host inventory file?

Summary

In this chapter, you learned how to create multiple environments that map to the software development workflow or the phases. We started with a brief overview of inventory groups and inventory variables, specifically, the `group_vars` file. This was followed by the two approaches used to manage environments. Finally, we refactored our code, went on to create the `dev` environment, and tested it by overriding one variable from the environment. In the next chapter, you are going to learn about infrastructure orchestration and how Ansible shines when it comes to orchestrating complex infrastructure workflows, zero downtime deployments, and so on.

10
Orchestrating Infrastructure with Ansible

Orchestration can mean different things at different times when used in different scenarios. The following are some of the orchestration scenarios described:

- Running ad hoc commands in parallel on a group of hosts, for example, using a `for` loop to walk over a group of web servers to restart the Apache service. This is the crudest form of orchestration.

- Invoking an orchestration engine to launch another configuration management tool to enforce correct ordering.

- Configuring a multitier application infrastructure in a certain order with the ability to have fine-grained control over each step, and the flexibility to move back and forth while configuring multiple components. For example, installing the database, setting up the web server, coming back to the database, creating a schema, going to web servers to start services, and more.

Most real-world scenarios are similar to the last scenario, which involve a multitier application stacks and more than one environment, where it's important to bring up and update nodes in a certain order, and in a coordinated way. It's also useful to actually test that the application is up and running before moving on to the next. The workflow to set up the stack for the first time versus pushing updates can be different. There can be times when you would not want to update all the servers at once, but do them in batches so that downtime is avoided.

In this chapter, we will cover the following topics:

- Orchestration scenarios
- Using Ansible as an infrastructure orchestrating engine
- Implementing rolling updates
- Using tags, limits and patterns
- Building tests into playbooks

Ansible as an orchestrator

When it comes to orchestration of any sort, Ansible really shines over other tools. Of course, as the creators of Ansible would say, it's more than a configuration management tool, which is true. Ansible can find a place for itself in any of the orchestration scenarios discussed earlier. It was designed to manage complex multitier deployments. Even if you have your infrastructure being automated with other configuration management tools, you can consider Ansible to orchestrate those.

Let's discuss the specific features that Ansible ships with, which are useful for orchestration.

Multiple playbooks and ordering

Unlike most other configuration management systems, Ansible supports running different playbooks at different times to configure or manage the same infrastructure. You can create one playbook to set up the application stack for the first time, and another to push updates over time in a certain manner. Another property of the playbook is that it can contain more than one play, which allows the separation of groups of hosts for each tier in the application stack, and configures them at the same time.

Pre-tasks and post-tasks

We have used pre-tasks and post-tasks earlier, which are very relevant while orchestrating, as these allow us to execute a task or run validations before and after running a play. Let's use the example of updating web servers that are registered with the load balancer. Using pre-tasks, a web server can be taken out of a load balancer, then the role is applied to the web servers to push updates, followed by post-tasks which register the web server back to the load balancer. Moreover, if these servers are being monitored by **Nagios**, alerts can be disabled during the update process and automatically enabled again using pre-tasks and post-tasks. This can avoid the noise that the monitoring tool may generate in the form of alerts.

Delegation

If you would like tasks to be selectively run on a certain class of hosts, especially the ones outside the current play, the delegation feature of Ansible can come in handy. This is relevant to the scenarios discussed previously and is commonly used with pre-tasks and post-tasks. For example, before updating a web server, it needs to be deregistered from the load balancer. Now, this task should be run on the load balancer, which is not part of the play. This dilemma can be solved by using the delegation feature. With pre-tasks, a script can be launched on the load balancer using the `delegate_to` keyword, which does the deregistering part as follows:

```
- name: deregister web server from lb
  shell: < script to run on lb host >
  delegate_to: lbIf there areis more than one load balancers,
  anan inventory group can be iterated over as, follows:

- name: deregister web server from lb
  shell: < script to run on lb host >
  delegate_to: "{{ item }}"
  with_items: groups.lb
```

Rolling updates

This is also called batch updates or zero-downtime updates. Let's assume that we have 100 web servers that need to be updated. If we define these in an inventory and launch a playbook against them, Ansible will start updating all the hosts in parallel. This can also cause downtime. To avoid complete downtime and have a seamless update, it would make sense to update them in batches, for example, 20 at a time. While running a playbook, batch size can be mentioned by using the `serial` keyword in the play. Let's take a look at the following code snippet:

```
- hosts: www
  remote_user: vagrant
  sudo: yes
  serial: 20
```

Tests

While orchestrating, it's not only essential to configure the applications in order, but also to ensure that they are actually started, and functioning as expected. Ansible modules, such as `wait_for` and `uri`, help you build that testing into the playbooks, for example:

```
- name: wait for mysql to be up
  wait_for: host=db.example.org port=3106 state=started
```

```
- name: check if a uri returns content
  uri: url=http://{{ inventory_hostname }}/api
  register: apicheck
```

The `wait_for` module can be additionally used to test the existence of a file. It's also useful when you would like to wait until a service is available before proceeding.

Tags

Ansible plays map roles to specific hosts. While the plays are run, the entire logic that is called from the main task is executed. While orchestrating, we may need to just run a part of the tasks based on the phases that we want to bring the infrastructure in. One example is a zookeeper cluster, where it's important to bring up all the nodes in the cluster at the same time, or in a gap of a few seconds. Ansible can orchestrate this easily with a two-phase execution. In the first phase, you can install and configure the application on all nodes, but not start it. The second phase involves starting the application on all nodes almost simultaneously. This can be achieved by tagging individual tasks, for example, configure, install, service, and more.

For example, let's take a look at the following screenshot:

```
- name: install haproxy
  apt:
    name: "{{ haproxy['pkg'] }}"
  tags:
    - install          ⬅ tag
```

While running a playbook, all tasks with a specific tag can be called using `--tags` as follows:

```
$ Ansible-playbook -i customhosts site.yml --tags install
```

Tags can not only be applied to tasks, but also to the roles, as follows:

```
{ role: nginx, when: Ansible_os_family == 'Debian', tags: 'www' }
```

If a specific task needs to be executed always, even if filtered with a tag, use a special tag called `always`. This will make the task execute unless an overriding option, such as `--skip-tags always` is used.

Patterns and limits

Limits can be used to run tasks on a subset of hosts, which are filtered by patterns. For example, the following code would run tasks only on hosts that are part of the db group:

```
$ Ansible-playbook -i customhosts site.yml --limit db
```

Patterns usually contain a group of hosts to include or exclude. A combination of more than one pattern can be specified as follows:

```
$ Ansible-playbook -i customhosts site.yml --limit db,lb
```

Having a colon as separator can be used to filter hosts further. The following command would run tasks on all hosts except for the ones that belong to the groups www and db:

```
$ Ansible-playbook -i customhosts site.yml --limit 'all:!www:!db'
```

Note that this usually needs to be enclosed in quotes. In this pattern, we used the all group, which matches all hosts in the inventory, and can be replaced with *. That was followed by ! to exclude hosts in the db group. The output of this command is as follows, which shows that plays by the name db and www were skipped as no hosts matched due to the filter we used previously:

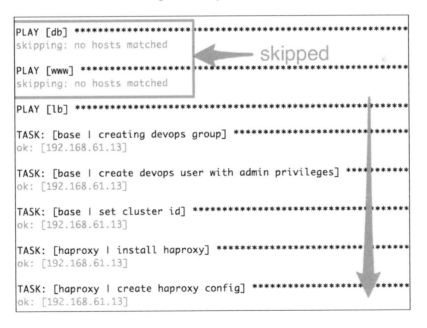

Let's now see these orchestration features in action. We will begin by tagging the role and do the multiphase execution followed by writing a new playbook to manage updates to the WordPress application.

Tagging the roles

Let's now start tagging the roles we created earlier. We will create the following tags that map to the phases the applications are managed in:

- Install
- Configure
- Start

Here is an example of adding tags to the `haproxy` role. Tagging other roles is excluded from the text to avoid redundancy. We can either add tags to the tasks inside the role or tag the complete roles in a playbook. Let's begin by tagging tasks:

```
---
# filename: roles/haproxy/tasks/install.yml
  - name: install haproxy
    apt:
      name: "{{ haproxy['pkg'] }}"
    tags:
      - install
```

```
---
# filename: roles/haproxy/tasks/configure.yml
 - name: create haproxy config
    template: src="haproxy.cfg.j2" dest="{{
    haproxy['config']['cnfpath'] }}" mode=0644
    notify:
     - restart haproxy service
    tags:
     - configure

 - name: enable haproxy
    template: src="haproxy.default.j2" dest=/and
    more/default/haproxy mode=0644
    notify:
     - restart haproxy service
    tags:
     - configure
```

```
---
# filename: roles/haproxy/tasks/service.yml
  - name: start haproxy server
    service:
      name: "{{ haproxy['service'] }}"
      state: started
    tags:
      - start
```

After tagging tasks in a role, we will additionally tag the roles in the playbooks too, as follows:

```
# filename: db.yml
  roles:
- { role: mysql, tags: 'mysql' }

#filename: www.yml
  roles:
    - { role: nginx, when: Ansible_os_family == 'Debian', tags: [
    'www', 'nginx' ] }
    - { role: php5-fpm, tags: [ 'www', 'php5-fpm' ] }
    - { role: wordpress, tags: [ 'www', 'wordpress' ] }

#filename: lb.yml
  roles:
- { role: haproxy, when: Ansible_os_family == 'Debian', tags:
  'haproxy' }
```

Once applied, the tags for our main playbook can be listed as follows:

```
$ Ansible-playbook -i customhosts site.yml --list-tags
```

```
#Output:

playbook: site.yml

  play #1 (db): TAGS: []
    TASK TAGS: [configure, install, mysql, start]

  play #2 (www): TAGS: []
    TASK TAGS: [configure, install, nginx, php5-fpm, ssl, start,
wordpress, www]

  play #3 (lb): TAGS: []
    TASK TAGS: [configure, haproxy, install, start]
```

Using the combination of tags and limits gives us a fine-grained control over what gets executed in a playbook run, for example:

```
# Run install tasks for haproxy,
$ Ansible-playbook -i customhosts site.yml --tags=install --limit lb
```

```
# Install and configure all but web servers
$ Ansible-playbook -i customhosts site.yml --tags=install,configure
--limit 'all:!www'


# Run all tasks with tag nginx
$ Ansible-playbook -i customhosts site.yml --tags=nginx
```

Creating an orchestration playbook for WordPress

We have a site-wide playbook, that is, the `site.yml` file that serves us to install and configure the complete WordPress stack. For updating the application with zero downtime and deploying new revisions, the `site.yml` file is not the ideal playbook though. We would want to follow a workflow that would involve the following steps:

1. Update the web servers one at a time. This will avoid any downtime.

2. Before updating, deregister the web server from the haproxy load balancer. This will stop the traffic to the web server in order to avoid downtime.

3. Run roles related to the WordPress application, that is, Nginx, php5-fpm, and WordPress.

4. Ensure that the web server is running and is listening to port 80.

5. Register the server back on haproxy and start sending the traffic again.

Let's create a playbook by the name `update.yml`, which does the orchestration just as explained earlier and uses most of the features discussed previously in this chapter. Here is the playbook:

```
  ---
# Playbook for updating web server in batches
# filename: update_www.yml
- hosts: www
  remote_user: vagrant
  sudo: yes
  serial: 1
  pre_tasks:
    - name: deregister web server from  load balancer
    shell: echo "disable server fifanews/{{ Ansible_hostname }}" |
    socat stdio /var/lib/haproxystats
    delegate_to: "{{ item }}"
    with_items: groups.lb
```

```
roles:
  - { role: nginx, when: Ansible_os_family == 'Debian' }
  - php5-fpm
  - wordpress
post_tasks:
  - name: wait for web server to come up
  wait_for: host={{ inventory_hostname }} port=80 state=started
  - name: register webserver from  load balancer
  shell: echo "enable server fifanews/{{ Ansible_hostname }}" |
  socat stdio /var/lib/haproxystats
  delegate_to: "{{ item }}"
  with_items: groups.lb
```

Let's analyze this code:

- The playbook contains just one play, which runs on the hosts that belong to the www group in inventory.

- The serial keyword specifies the batch size, and allows rolling updates with zero downtime. In our case, since we have fewer hosts, we chose one web server to be updated at a time.

- Before applying the role, the host is deregistered from the load balancer using the pre-tasks section ,which runs a shell command with **socat**. This is run on all load balancers using the delegate keyword. Socat is a Unix utility similar to and more at (nc) but has a richer feature set.

- After deregistering the host, roles are applied to it; this will update the configurations for the web server or deploy new code.

- Once updated, the post-tasks kick in, which first wait until the web server is up and listening to port 80, and only after its ready, then it registers it back to the load balancer.

Review questions

Do you think you've understood the chapter well enough? Try answering the following questions to test your understanding:

1. Is it possible to use Ansible to orchestrate another configuration management tool?

2. How can you achieve zero downtime while deploying applications with Ansible?

3. What does the --limit command do to Ansible playbook?

4. How would you run a subset of tasks for a given role in a playbook?

5. What is the purpose of using pre-tasks and post-tasks?

6. What modules can be used to run tests from playbooks?

7. Why is the `always` tag special?

Summary

We started this chapter by discussing what orchestration is, what different orchestration scenarios are, and how Ansible can fit in. You learned about Ansible's set of rich features in the context or orchestration. This includes multi-playbook support, pre-tasks and post-tasks, tags and limits, running tests, and a lot more. We went on to tag the roles we created earlier and learned how to control what portion of code runs on which machines using a combination of tags, patterns, and limits. Finally, we created a new playbook to orchestrate the workflow to update web servers, which involves zero-downtime deployment, delegation, pre-tasks and post-tasks, and tests. You also learned that Ansible can be a good fit in any orchestration scenario.

This brings us to the end of this book. Before we conclude, on behalf of the reviewers, editors, contributors, and rest of the publishing team, I would like to thank you for considering this book as a companion in your journey towards being an Ansible practitioner.

We hope that by now you have become comfortable with the various primitives that Ansible offers to automate common infrastructure tasks, create dynamic roles, manage multitier application configurations, zero-downtime deployments, orchestrate complex infrastructure, and more. We hope that you will be able to apply the knowledge acquired in this book to create effective Ansible playbooks.

References

For more information regarding Ansible, refer to the following URLs:

- **The Ansible documentation**: `http://docs.ansible.com/`
- **The Jinja2 template documentation**: `http://jinja.pocoo.org/docs/dev/`
- **Ansible Example Playbooks**: `https://github.com/ansible/ansible-examples`
- **Ansible MySQL Roles by Benno Joy and Jeff Geerling**:
  - `https://github.com/bennojoy/mysql`
  - `https://github.com/geerlingguy/ansible-role-mysql`
- **Ansible Nginx Role by Benno Joy and DAUPHANT Julien**: `https://github.com/jdauphant/ansible-role-nginx`
- **Multistage Environments with Ansible**: `http://rosstuck.com/multistage-environments-with-ansible/`
- **Ansible project's Google group thread on how to create Ansible environments**: `https://groups.google.com/forum/#!topic/ansible-project/jd3cuR7rqCE`
- **Caching Facts in Ansible by Jan-Piet Mens**: `http://jpmens.net/2015/01/29/caching-facts-in-ansible/`
- **Orchestration, You keep Using that Word by Michael DeHaan**: `http://www.ansible.com/blog/orchestration-you-keep-using-that-word`

Index

events
    automating, with handlers 32, 33

F

facts
    about 41, 79, 80
    accessing, for non-playbook hosts 105-107
    caching, in files 107, 108
FastCGI Process Manager (FPM) 89

G

git 109

H

handlers
    used, for automating actions 32, 33
    used, for automating events 32, 33
hash
    creating 92
    iterating 93, 94
    nested hashes 92, 93
Htop 12

I

idempotence
    about 18
    of command modules, controlling 71
include statements 24

J

Jinja2 templates
    about 40
    conditional control 83
    formation 40
    MySQL template, updating 84

L

limits 135
load balancer role
    creating 100-105

M

magic variables
    about 100
    group_names 100
    groups 100
    hostvars 100
    inventory_hostname 100
    play_hosts 100
metadata
    adding, to role 49, 50
modules
    about 17
    and idempotence 18
MySQL databases
    creating 91
MySQL role
    about 48
    adding, to DB servers 57
    hashes, merging 81
    metadata, adding 49, 50
    multilevel variable dictionaries 80
    refactoring 80
    scaffolding creating, Ansible-Galaxy
        used 48, 49
    server, configuring 82
    variables, using in handlers 50, 51
    variables, using in tasks 50, 51
MySQL template
    updating 84

N

nested playbook 25
nesting 24, 25
Nginx
    configurations, templating 44-47
    PHP site information, defining 94-96
    SSL support, adding 117-119
    virtual hosts, creating 94
Nginx role
    creating 29
    dependencies, adding 30
    files, managing for 30, 31
non-playbook hosts
    facts, accessing for 105-107

W

when statements
  about 78, 79
  fact-based selection 79
with statement 87, 88
WordPress
  application, deploying 69, 70
  command modules, idempotence
      controlling 71, 72
  configuring 73-75
  extracting, with shell module 72, 73
  installing 70, 71
  installing, URL 70
  orchestration playbook, creating 138, 139
  requisites, configuring 88
  variables registered 72
www playbook
  creating 26
  custom role paths 27
  roles, parameterizing 27

Y

YAML 12

Z

zero downtime updates 133

Thank you for buying
Ansible Playbook Essentials

About Packt Publishing

Packt, pronounced 'packed', published its first book, *Mastering phpMyAdmin for Effective MySQL Management*, in April 2004, and subsequently continued to specialize in publishing highly focused books on specific technologies and solutions.

Our books and publications share the experiences of your fellow IT professionals in adapting and customizing today's systems, applications, and frameworks. Our solution-based books give you the knowledge and power to customize the software and technologies you're using to get the job done. Packt books are more specific and less general than the IT books you have seen in the past. Our unique business model allows us to bring you more focused information, giving you more of what you need to know, and less of what you don't.

Packt is a modern yet unique publishing company that focuses on producing quality, cutting-edge books for communities of developers, administrators, and newbies alike. For more information, please visit our website at www.packtpub.com.

About Packt Open Source

In 2010, Packt launched two new brands, Packt Open Source and Packt Enterprise, in order to continue its focus on specialization. This book is part of the Packt Open Source brand, home to books published on software built around open source licenses, and offering information to anybody from advanced developers to budding web designers. The Open Source brand also runs Packt's Open Source Royalty Scheme, by which Packt gives a royalty to each open source project about whose software a book is sold.

Writing for Packt

We welcome all inquiries from people who are interested in authoring. Book proposals should be sent to author@packtpub.com. If your book idea is still at an early stage and you would like to discuss it first before writing a formal book proposal, then please contact us; one of our commissioning editors will get in touch with you.

We're not just looking for published authors; if you have strong technical skills but no writing experience, our experienced editors can help you develop a writing career, or simply get some additional reward for your expertise.

Ansible Configuration Management

ISBN: 978-1-78328-081-0   Paperback: 92 pages

Leverage the power of Ansible to quickly configure your Linux infrastructure with ease

1. Starts with the most simple usage of Ansible and builds on that.

2. Shows how to use Ansible to configure your Linux machines.

3. Teaches how to extend Ansible to add features you need.

4. Explains techniques for using Ansible in large, complex environments.

Learning Ansible

ISBN: 978-1-78355-063-0   Paperback: 308 pages

Use Ansible to configure your systems, deploy software, and orchestrate advanced IT tasks

1. Use Ansible to automate your infrastructure effectively, with minimal effort.

2. Customize and consolidate your configuration management tools with the secure and highly-reliable features of Ansible.

3. Unleash the abilities of Ansible and extend the functionality of your mainframe system through the use of powerful, real-world examples.

Creating Development Environments with Vagrant

Second Edition

ISBN: 978-1-78439-702-9   Paperback: 156 pages

Leverage the power of Vagrant to create and manage virtual development environments with Puppet, Chef, and VirtualBox

1. Get your projects up and running quickly and effortlessly by simulating complicated environments that can be easily shared with colleagues.

2. Provision virtual machines using Puppet, Ansible, and Chef.

3. A practical, hands-on guide that helps you learn how to create powerful and flexible virtual development environments.

Vagrant Virtual Development Environment Cookbook

ISBN: 978-1-78439-374-8   Paperback: 250 pages

Over 35 hands-on recipes to help you master Vagrant, and create and manage virtual computational environments

1. Configure and deploy software to Vagrant machines with scripts and configuration management tools.

2. Manage and share Vagrant development environments with cloud.

3. Packed with practical real-life examples to improve existing working systems.

Please check **www.PacktPub.com** for information on our titles

11108759R00095